THE END OF THE ARMISTICE

THE
END OF THE ARMISTICE

By
GILBERT KEITH CHESTERTON

Essay Index Reprint Series

BOOKS FOR LIBRARIES PRESS
FREEPORT, NEW YORK

First Published 1940
Reprinted 1970

STANDARD BOOK NUMBER:

8369-1644-1

LIBRARY OF CONGRESS CATALOG CARD NUMBER:

78-117767

PRINTED IN THE UNITED STATES OF AMERICA

COMPILER'S NOTE

A word of explanation is needed as to how this book came to be. I was reading through a mass of Chesterton essays with the idea of selecting enough of them to make a book rather like *The Thing*. But I had not been reading long before I realised that, as far back as the middle twenties and continuously up to his death in 1936, his mind had been dominated by the present war. It is scarcely too much to say that he took it for granted as a simple fact of future history. That is to say he saw it not as possible, nor as probable, but as a thing already on the way and humanly speaking certain to arrive. He saw how it would arrive—Germany would attack Poland; he saw closer still, that Germany would do so in agreement with Russia. "The Prussian patriot may plaster himself all over with eagles and crosses, but he will be found in practice side by side with the Red Flag. The Prussian and the Russian will agree about everything; especially about Poland."

Now when a man is as right as that in his forecasts, there is some reason to think he may be right in his premises. That is why I have sorted out and

Compiler's Note

arranged these essays[1] as his analysis of the whole problem of Germany in Europe. They were written at various dates, not in any particular order nor as chapters of a future book. Yet they form a unity because of the unity in his own mind. He had certain very clear principles and in their light he wrote of things as they happened: the year does not matter because he held his view steadily throughout. He had formed a certain theory of Germany—part of a larger theory of Europe—and everything that happened from 1914 to his death in 1936 confirmed it; though not so spectacularly as it has been confirmed by all that has happened since.

What the theory is appears fully in the essays themselves, but I give it here in skeleton in order to explain the plan of the book. There is a reality called Europe, which makes sense when you see it as Christendom. To this reality Germany belongs and Prussia does not belong. The problem for Europe is the healing of Germany by the exorcising of Prussianism; and this, to vary the metaphor, means some sort of uprooting. If racial arrogance

[1] I have made a few excisions where the original essay dealt with matters not on this main theme; and once or twice I have joined together parts of different essays. It also seemed advisable to add a few footnotes where the context did not make clear what incident the author was referring to.

6

had been first taught to the Germans by Hitler, the problem of uprooting it would be less grave, for Hitler is too new to have struck deep root. But it is a thing long growing and its roots are centuries deep. That is why the first section of this book is on Prussianism. There is a force there which by its very nature is an abiding trouble to Germany and so to the world. Prussia might conceivably be converted by a real religious conversion; otherwise it must be restrained. And to be restrained it must be understood. If we misconceive its nature, we shall repeat the mistake of Versailles—we shall build our dams in the wrong places.

Following the section on Prussianism comes the group of essays on Hitlerism. What is best done here is the analysis of the heresy of Race, showing that the world can never be at peace while that heresy remains unbroken: since it means " everlastingly looking for your countrymen in other people's countries ". The ordinary patriot is a kind of watchdog, guarding his own gate: " but if patriots are trained as a pack of hounds, to follow a scent blown upon any breeze, to go through all fences and across all fields, they are trained in a certain spirit which is quite certainly of some peril to their neighbours ".

Compiler's Note

The third section is a small group of essays on Poland, " the long sword-blade between the Byzantine tradition of Muscovy and the materialism of Prussia ".

The final section—" Pacifism and Cynicism "— may be regarded either as completing the picture or as a companion picture. While Europe was moving so steadily in a direction, what was England doing? In this section, against the clear steadiness of Chesterton's mind, we see the kaleidoscope of English public opinion. Indeed " opinion " is too rational-sounding a word for what was simply a series of moods, one melting into the next but all making for passivity in face of the growing movement in Germany which surely at every moment bore upon its face the precise promise of what its maturity would mean to us.

There is no need to say everything in a note of this sort. But there is one further element so close to the foundation of Chesterton's thought that even a summary might be held seriously misleading without it. I can come to it best by considering a question often raised against us—by what right does England, whose own history is not stainless, now oppose Prussia? The question will not stand a moment's reflection, for it implies that a nation which has done wrong must never be allowed to resist wrong.

Compiler's Note

England, for instance, has persecuted Ireland, therefore she must not try to save Poland from persecution. She must, in short, be so paralysed by conscience that she will leave the world at the mercy of the conscienceless. The fallacy is plain and the answer is plain : the way to atone for doing wrong is not to do nothing but to do right. Now Chesterton, as the reader will discover for himself, was too clear-headed to see the war of the Allies against Prussia as a war of angels against devils. No patriot ever had a clearer vision of his own country's crimes. His answer to the question was twofold. First, he did, as the reader will see, hold that there were special elements in the crimes of Prussia which made them a threat to the world in a sense in which the crimes of England or France or Italy were not. But this, he knew, was a point on which men might honestly hold another view. His second answer was different : it was a question : In face of a crime being committed here and now, how should England act ? The balance of right and wrong over the long span of the past is a delicate one; but its delicacy must not prevent us considering what is the right thing to do *now*, in this or that concrete situation ? When a small ally is being violated, you do not ask, " Am I worthy to go to her aid ? " When evil threatens

Compiler's Note

all your world, you do not ask, " Am I worthy to
resist it ? " One is always worthy to do right.

I have said that Chesterton foresaw this war. His
one haunting fear was that England might not be
in it. Now, we may hope, he knows.

F. J. SHEED.

CONTENTS

11

Contents

3. Poland

4. Pacifism and Cynicism

Epilogue

INTRODUCTORY

I

ARMS AND THE ARMISTICE

ANYTHING that I write on the subject of the Armistice will be most improper; and even indecent. The most horrid thing about it is that it will really be about the Armistice. For the first fact to be noted, about this date and celebration, is the rather remarkable fact of the name itself. For, you will notice, it has never at any time been called The Peace. After much more than a decade, during which the nations have in the main been practically peaceful, we still do not call it The Peace. We still speak of it by a special and separate term which means The Truce. The world, weary of war as it has hardly ever been weary in all the ages, yet has an instinct guiding even its language, and it has never in all that time dared finally to announce Peace with Prussia. It only celebrates annually, with any number of sincere prayers and hopes for peace, the Armistice with Prussia. And if anybody thinks that the world was very wrong to feel like this, or that I am very wrong to put it into plain words, let him look at Prussia to-day and see.

In this matter I belong to a small group or school in England, which may now possibly be listened to

15

again; or rather begin for the first time to be listened
to at all. We were in a special state of obscurity and
insignificance; for we were a minority swallowed up
in a majority. That is, we agreed with our countrymen about the rightness of fighting, but we almost
entirely disagreed with them about the reasons for
doing it. We were, I hope, good Englishmen, and
in that at least at one with other Englishmen. But
we also were, or wanted to be, good Europeans;
and most Englishmen did not even know what being
a good European meant. Consequently, too many
of the politicians, publicists and pressmen of that
country had rather the air of going to war with
Germany first and making up the reasons for it
afterwards. Some of them really were made up; in
the sense of merely manufactured by unscrupulous
propagandists. Some of them were lies; some of
them were ludicrous and transparent lies. They
were rapidly invented by hustling, hard-headed,
practical publicity-agents; so they were equally
rapidly exploded or exposed. But we had nothing
to do with all this; we were content to stick to the
real reasons; and the real reasons were not lies.
They were truths of history and philosophy; parts
of the fundamental structure of European civilisation. We never said that all Germans bayoneted

babies. We knew there were quite as many good-natured people in various parts of Germany as anywhere else, or perhaps more. We never said the Prussian militaristic government boiled the bodies of its own soldiers to turn them into glue, or some such substance. We should have said, if anything, that the Prussian militarists were capable of any crime *except* boiling the bodies of soldiers into glue. We never joined in the journalistic slanders of those who, being big-business men and practical organisers of the modern world, had of course no notion of what the War was all about. We never uttered any of the newspaper nonsense that described the average German as a lawless fiend let loose on the earth and capable of doing anything. We should be more likely to say that he was a meek, mild, obedient person, incapable of doing anything, except what he was told to do. The real question was, not merely even what he was told to do, but (above all) who told him to do it. The answer to that is a fundamental fact of modern history, and explains, among other things, why we talk of the Armistice and not the Peace.

What we said before the War and during the War, what we said during the pacifist reaction against the War, what we say now during the reaction against the pacifist reaction, has nothing to do with news-

paper stunts or even with national passions. It is
something not only older than the newspapers, but
older than the nations; it was there when the political
parties had no labels and even most of the peoples
no names. As a man may say, as a scientific fact, that
there is in Northern China a well of petroleum, we
said that there is in Northern Europe a fountain of
poison. It is a fact; and it continues to flow. It is
obviously nonsense to call it Germany. It is not
really satisfactory even to call it Prussia. It is much
more satisfactory simply to call it Pride.

It is a thing of the spirit; it is not a nation; it
is a heresy. It is an ideal outside the European ideal;
outside what most of us would call the normal human
ideal. It is something alien to Europe, which Europe
cannot digest and did not destroy. It is difficult to
find a fit word for it; for all the right words were
used in the wrong way by the mere propaganda of
the War. Any rich newspaper proprietor could
describe the Prussians as Barbarians; but it was not
enlightening, because he was a barbarian himself,
and a bounder as well. The nearest definition I
know is this. The civilised man, like the religious
man, is one who recognises the strange and irritating
fact that something exists besides himself. What
Jefferson called, with his fine restraint, "a decent

respect for the opinion of mankind " ; what medieval people called Christendom or the judgment of all Christian princes ; what any Christian will call the conscience of man as a witness to the justice of God ; that, in one form or another, does everywhere affect civilised people. An Agnostic may hesitate about giving it the name of God. An American may very reasonably hesitate about giving it the name of the League of Nations. But in one way or other, that is the test; that the man does not think his dignity lowered by admitting a general law, though it may go against him.

Now we thought, and think, and are now a thousand times confirmed in thinking, that there does really lie to the north-east, between us and the Christian State of Poland and the almost Asiatic State of Muscovy, a real independent source or spring of the opposite spirit. It is not only something that praises itself; it is something that needs no praise except its own. It is futile and confusing to quarrel about labels, like ' nationalism ' or ' patriotism '. We are talking about different things. A Frenchman is proud of France. But a Prussian is not proud of Prussia; he is simply proud, because he is a Prussian. He is not proud, like a French Crusader, of what his country has done for Christendom. He is not proud, like a French Revolutionist, of what his country has done for humanity. He is simply proud of himself and his sort; and would be equally proud of their wrecking Christendom or enslaving humanity. This is the problem of Prussia, which is not even the problem of Prussians but only of Prussianism. It is certainly not the problem of Germans; though it is partly the problem of the limits they have accepted and the leadership they have obeyed. But the point of it is that something unbaptised and barbaric does remain among the nations; as it would say, unconquered; as we should say, unconverted; and, anyhow, entirely unrepentant. That is the problem of the last loud and hysterical outbreak in Germany. It is not the things they say; it is not even the things they do; it is most certainly not the thing they are most blamed for doing. Many of the things the new Germans are saying are quite true. But they do not say that the truths are true; they only say they are German. Many of the things they do are right. But they do not say they are right; they say they are German. That is, they do not refer to, or recognise, any standard outside themselves. When they say they worship the German God, they really mean that they would not be judged, even on the Day of Judgment, by any god who was not a German. But the Founder of Christianity and Christendom neglected to make Himself a German.

The world, very unwisely, allowed this unnatural thing to grow stronger and stronger in Europe throughout the nineteenth century. It was nearly cut short by Napoleon at Jena; it could easily have been checked when it began to steal from Poland and Denmark and France. It was allowed to grow so enormously strong that it took the strength of four nations to inflict on it a belated and a badly-managed defeat. The defeat was badly managed, because the victors did not understand what they were fighting. They went by labels again, and thought they were fighting a nation when they were fighting a notion—but a notion that was a nightmare. They treated a human place like Hungary worse than an inhuman place like Prussia. They did not understand (what every fact is now proving every day) that Austria is not the ally of Prussia, but the chief antagonist of Prussia. The Allies were right and did not know it; and they did almost everything that was wrong; with the one exception that they restored Poland. The French atheists nearly lost Alsace again by their blind and blundering old prejudices against Christianity. The English idiotic-ally insisted on still torturing Ireland with Black and Tans, immediately after having won a war for small

The End of the Armistice

nationalities. They made every mistake they possibly could; but then again, you must remember that their policy was managed by practical business men.

But for all that, they were right; and to-day, on this solemn anniversary of the Armistice, they are clearly and finally proved right. There is that fountain of poisonous pride, there is that isolated idolatry of self, which they set out to destroy; and the chief point against them is that they did not destroy it enough. Perhaps the answer is that it was an idea, and could only have been conquered by another idea; and modern politicians have no ideas. Perhaps the Pacifists are so far right, that the final cure will be found in conversion and not in conquest; and that missionaries may be found who will talk to these perverted Pagans as others talked to the barbarian chiefs of the Dark Ages. On all this I do not here attempt to pronounce. I do not say that the Armistice will be only an Armistice; though nobody has ever called it anything else. I do not say that the prayers and thoughts of thousands of sane people may not yet turn it into a real and permanent Peace. But I do say that recent events in Germany have revealed as with a floodlight the essential fact in which many brave men only had believed, even when they fought and died for it. And

Arms and the Armistice

that fact is a brute fact of psychology; that almost all other men have been taught in some vague traditional way to appeal to some truth that is not subjective (a favourite German word); that they have been taught either to appeal to God or to appeal to Man; but the Germans have been taught only to appeal to Germany.

Such are the depressing, nay degrading and deplorable sentiments that are immediately awakened in *my* mind, by the mention and memory of the Armistice. How different from those exalted and optimistic affirmations of the immediate and inevitable appearance of Peace, Perfect Peace, among all the peoples of the earth, those silver trumpets of eloquence praising the uninterrupted triumphs of the League of Nations; those visions of happy fatalism showing the now complete and final disappearance of every weapon from the world; those radiant sermons on Love and Brotherhood and Unity, which have in late years been poured out so copiously by the great and wise, and especially the wealthy; and all those who think that a war should never be waged except very occasionally, for money, against a small and defenceless State. Many of these moralists will add that, even then, it is more truly Christian to starve the people to death by some economic boycott or blockade, rather than sink to the cynical level

The End of the Armistice

of risking our own lives in order to kill them. In all these higher moral sentiments I feel I shall be found sadly wanting; and, having been particularly asked to write an article upon the Armistice, I fear I cannot write anything except what the Armistice really means to me. And the Armistice, strangely enough, does not mean to me any shame in those of my friends and kindred who died in arms. It does not instantly come natural to me to celebrate the anniversary of their victory by shrieking that they died in vain, or to seek to avoid a repetition of their deaths merely by laboriously proving that they were as bad as their enemies. Hoping for peace, like all the world, I will not express my compassion for courageous men by writing foul psychological novels to prove that they were all cowards; nor do I hold the new dramatic canon that the way to exalt tragedy is to deprive it of dignity. But I am none the less vividly conscious that the next tragedy of that type will be even more tragic. I am all the more anxious to avert such disaster falling again upon the world; now that I know that my friends and brethren are henceforth doomed to suffer twice for the crime of patriotism; to be destroyed by their enemies and then despised by their countrymen.

Let us, therefore, for this and many other reasons,

join with all those who would make the Armistice
a festival and a prophecy of Peace. The Pacifists are
right in insisting that Peace, like War, is made by
the will of man; and they are therefore right in
adding that a moral responsibility in the matter lies
on all sorts and conditions of men. Where they are
generally wrong is, first, in assuming that all those
who anticipate War necessarily approve of War, or
even actually desire it; and, second, in supposing
that those who did approve of a particular War
necessarily approved of it for the particular reasons
given by the richest or most successful rascals in
journalism or commercial politics. They will have to
think a great deal more clearly and honestly than that,
if we are to avoid war or even escape out of it alive if
it comes. And clear and honest thinking must not
shrink from starting afresh with that first fact, which
is still a final fact, that there is in Christendom, unconverted and unconquered, a force that is not Christian.
Surely it is not so very impossible to believe that it was
this that threatened the world with war in 1914; when
it is obviously this that threatens it with war now?

But for us, who celebrate the Armistice, there is
surely a nobler and more humane way of celebrating
it. Let us forget for a day whatever we may think
about the faults of others; and pray that we may

not again wreck the hope of the world by faults of our own. Let us pray that if the challenge does indeed come again, we may not meet it by random slander or roaring self-righteousness; that we may test the quarrel by the history of nations as studied by sincere and serious men, and not by nonsense made up in a newspaper-office on a principle of inverted advertisement; or the theory that propagandists may say anything so long as it is abuse, as salesmen may say anything so long as it is flattery. Let us pray to be delivered from the vices and vulgarities of our own civilisation; and all the more if we sincerely believe that it is still a civilisation, and may need to be defended from something that is still a savagery. It is a fine thing to be swift to forgive our enemies; but it is a finer thing not to be too eager to forgive ourselves. If the ruin that fell on the great House of Hohenzollern was, as I still believe, a doom earned and provoked by the dehumanised pride of Prussia, we must not forget that the vast economic collapse that has affected the victors has almost as much of the quality of a great historical judgment; and the rebuke of fate to our own mercantile and mechanical culture. In so far as modern men can face such facts frankly, they will be worthy to find peace or fitted to face war.

PART I
PRUSSIANISM

II

THE EVIL FRIENDSHIP

ALL Christian history began with that great social occasion when Pilate and Herod shook hands. Hitherto, as everybody knew in Society circles, they had hardly been on speaking terms. Something led them to seek each other's support, a vague sense of social crisis, though very little was happening except the execution of an ordinary batch of criminals. The two rulers were reconciled on the very day when one of these convicts was crucified. That is what many people mean by Peace, and the substitution of a reign of Love for one of Hatred. Whether or no there is honour among thieves, there is always a certain social interdependence and solidarity among murderers ; and those sixteenth-century ruffians who conspired to assassinate Rizzio were always very careful to put their names, and especially each other's names, to what they called a " band ", so that at the worst they might all hang together. Many political friendships, nay even broad democratic comradeships, are of this nature ; and their representatives are really distressed when we decline to identify this

29

form of Love with the original mystical idea of Charity.

It sometimes seems to me that history is dominated and determined by these evil friendships. As all Christian history begins with the happy reconciliation of Herod and Pilate, so all modern history, in the recent revolutionary sense, begins with that strange friendship which ended in a quarrel, as the first quarrel had ended in a friendship. I mean that the two elements of destruction, which make the modern world more and more incalculable, were loosened with the light of that forgotten day when a lean French gentleman in a large wig, by name M. Arouet, travelled north with much annoyance to find the palace of a Prussian king, far away in the freezing Baltic plain. The strict title of the king in dynastic chronicles is Frederick the Second; but he is better known as Frederick the Great. The actual name of the Frenchman was Arouet, but he is better known as Voltaire.

The meeting of these two men, in the mid-winter of eighteenth-century scepticism and secularism, is a sort of spiritual marriage which brought forth the modern world; *monstrum horrendum informe ingens cui lumen ademptum*. But because that birth was monstrous and evil, and because true friendship and love are not evil, it did not come into the world to create one united thing, but two conflicting things, which between them were to shake the world to pieces. From Voltaire the Latins were to learn a raging scepticism. From Frederick the Teutons were to learn a raging pride. We may note at the start that neither of them cared very much about their own countries or traditions. Frederick was a German who refused even to learn German. Voltaire was a Frenchman who wrote a foul lampoon about Joan of Arc. They were cosmopolitans; they were not in any sense patriots. But there is this difference; that the patriot does, however stupidly, like the country; whereas the cosmopolitan does not in the least like the cosmos. They neither of them pretended to like anything very much. Voltaire was the more really humane of the two; but Frederick also could talk on occasion the cold humanitarianism that was the cant of his age. But Voltaire, even at his best, really began that modern mood that has blighted all the humanitarianism he honestly supported. He started the horrible habit of helping human beings only through pitying them and never through respecting them. Through him the oppression of the poor became a sort of cruelty to animals; and the loss of all that mystical sense that to wrong the image of God is to insult the ambassador of a King. Nevertheless, I believe that Voltaire had a heart; I think that Frederick was most heartless when he was most humane.

Anyhow, these two great sceptics met on the level, on the dead solid plain, as dull as the Baltic Plain; on the basis that there is no God, or no God who is concerned with men any more than with mites in cheese. On this basis they agreed; on this basis they disagreed; their quarrel was personal and trivial, but it ended by launching two European forces against each other, both rooted in the same unbelief. Voltaire said in effect, " I will show you that the sneers of a sceptic can produce a Revolution and a Republic and everywhere the overthrowing of thrones." And Frederick answered, "And I will show you that this same sneering scepticism can be used as easily to resist Reform, let alone Revolution; that scepticism can be the basis of support for the most tyrannical of thrones, for the bare brute domination of a master over his slaves." So they said farewell, and have since been sundered by two centuries of war; they said farewell, but presumably did not say " adieu ".

Of every such evil seed it may be noted that the seed is different from the flower, and the flower from the fruit. A demon of distortion always twists it

even out of its own unnatural nature. It may turn
into almost anything, except anything really good.
It is, to use the playful term of affection which Professor Freud applies to his baby, " a polymorphous
pervert ". These things not only do not produce the
special good they promise ; they do not produce even
the special evil they threaten. The Voltairean revolt
promised to produce, and even began to produce,
the rise of mobs and overthrow of thrones ; but it
was not the final form of scepticism. The actual
effect of what we call democracy has been the disappearance of the mob. We might say there were
mobs at the beginning of the Revolution and no
mobs at the end of it. That Voltairean influence has
not ended in the rule of mobs ; but in the rule of
secret societies. It has falsified politics throughout
the Latin world, till the recent Italian Counter-
Revolution. Voltaire has produced hypocritical and
pompous professional politicians, at whom he would
have been the first to jeer. But on his side, as I have
said, there does linger a certain humane and civilised
sentiment, which is not unreal. Only it is right to
remember what has really gone wrong on his side
of the Continental quarrel, when we are recording
the much wilder and wickeder wrong on the other
side of it.

The End of the Armistice

For the evil spirit of Frederick the Great has produced what might seem the very opposite evil. He who worshipped nothing has become a god who is quite blindly worshipped. He who cared nothing for Germany has become the battle-cry of madmen who care for nothing except Germany. He who was a cold cosmopolitan has heated seven times a hell of narrow national and tribal fury, which at this moment menaces mankind with a war that may be the end of the world. But the root of both perversions is in the common ground of atheist irresponsibility; there was nothing to stop the sceptic from turning democracy into secrecy; there was nothing to stop him interpreting liberty as the infinite licence of tyranny. The spiritual zero of Christendom was at that freezing instant when those two dry thin hatchet-faced men looked in each other's hollow eyes, and saw the sneer that was as eternal as the smile of a skull. Between them, they have nearly killed the thing by which we live.

These two points of peril or centres of unrest, the intellectual unrest of the Latins and the very unintellectual unrest of the Teutons, do doubtless both contribute to the instability of international relations; and threaten us all the more because they threaten each other. But when we have made every allowance for there being, in that sense, dangers on both sides, the main modern fact emerges, that the danger is mostly on one side; and that we have long been taught to look for it only on the other side. Much of Western opinion, especially English and American, has been trained to have a vague horror of Voltaire, often combined with a still vaguer respect for Frederick. No Wesleyans are likely to confuse Wesley with Voltaire. No Primitive Methodist is under the impression that Voltaire was a Primitive Methodist. But many such Protestant ministers really were under the impression that Frederick the Great was a Protestant Hero. None of them realised that Frederick was the greater atheist of the two. None of them certainly foresaw that Frederick, in the long run, would turn out to be the greater anarchist of the two. In short, nobody foresaw what everybody afterwards saw; the French Republic becoming a conservative force, and the Prussian Kingdom a purely destructive and lawless force. Victorians like Carlyle actually talked about pious Prussia, as if Blucher had been a saint or Moltke a mystic. General Goering may be trusted to teach us better; till we learn at last that nothing is so anarchical as discipline divorced from authority; that is, from right.

III

A NOTE ON DOLLFUSS

FOR about the last ten years we, being among the victors of the Great War, have been more or less grumbling at the peace which we ourselves imposed. And yet we have hardly ever grumbled at the one part of the settlement that was really wrong. On the contrary, we have taken a perverse pleasure in grumbling at the only parts of it that were really right. While we listened to all the spiteful stupidities of Prussian propaganda against Poland, we never noticed that we had left Prussia with a still more dangerous power of pressure, not only on South Germany, but on Austria. In other words, the one really big and bad blunder in the settlement was that we did not punish Prussianism in Prussia; we only punished it in Austria. Now it is true that the Austrian ultimatum to Serbia was a pure piece of Prussianism; whether or no it was dictated by Prussia. But in Austria the thing was incidental, was even accidental, was even partially provoked. In Prussia the thing is permanent; at any rate it is incessantly recurrent; as we have just recently discovered, with something like a jump.

A Note on Dollfuss

For about the last ten weeks we, being naturally concerned to keep some sort of peace in Europe, even, if necessary, the peace which we ourselves imposed, have woken up to the fact that the Prussia which we left relatively strong is again bullying the Austria which we left relatively weak. The just popularity of Dr. Dollfuss is not entirely founded on the joke that he is a small man; but upon the extremely serious fact that he now represents a small country. This is a case, however, in which quality is much more important than quantity. And one of the monstrous mistakes that the victorious Allies, or rather the politicians who represented them, really did make after the Great War, was a mistake concerning quality. It was an utter blindness and blundering ignorance about the *quality* of the culture of Austria. Men like President Wilson were brought up in a rather priggish culture, which taught them, among other things, that Kings are rather wicked; but that Emperors are even more wicked than Kings. Men like the French politicians were brought up in a much finer and more classical culture, but one which had very often an acrid anti-clerical prejudice, leading to a dislike of Austria on quite other and irrelevant grounds. Men like many of the English politicians were not brought up in any culture at all.

37

The End of the Armistice

All had a vague idea that as poor old Franz Joseph was an aged man with an Imperial crown and several sceptres, he must be even more " out-of-date " and backward and barbaric than the Kaiser with his several uniforms. What they did not understand is that traditional forms of Monarchy, whether good or bad, are not necessarily barbaric ; they are not even necessarily militaristic. And Vienna is not barbaric ; not even in the sense in which Berlin is barbaric.

If we never realised this before, it is time we realised it now ; and a good chance of realising it may be found in the duel of Dollfuss and Hitler. It is obvious in the very tone of the two men, when they talk to their respective followers. In most modern politics, unfortunately, it may truly be said that those who make history never know history. You can see that in the sort of history they make. And as one of our leading statesmen is said to have been under the impression that Cilicia and Silesia were the same place, it is not surprising that such statesmen did not know what any Middle-European could have told them about the difference in the tone and atmosphere of the Austrian Empire, as compared with either the Prussian or the Russian. The Austrian Empire had its faults, and, as I have said, even committed its crimes. But it was a world in which national types could live with some degree of liberality and ease; they were not all rolled out flat, as they were by the Kaisers and the Czars. The Poles, for instance, simply hated the Kaisers and the Czars; but they remained almost on amiable terms with a great many of the Austrians. Polish nobles stood high among the advisers of Austrian Emperors; so did Bohemian nobles. I knew a Bohemian aristocrat who was almost a fanatic for the national ideals of Bohemia; but it did not prevent him from being on polite terms with the Austrian Court, at which I believe he held some official position. In short, the Austrian Empire may have denied the nations independence, but it did not entirely deny them liberty. It was a relatively tolerant and tolerable government to live under; even for those who would naturally have preferred to live under no government but their own. And the reason, again, was a part of that history of the past which politicians will not read.

Prussia and Russia are very new powers; and they were tyrannical because they were new. There are modern methods of coercion and concentration that were utterly unknown to the loose feudal federations of the past. We all talk of the Prussian fighting-machine; and it was not altogether a fallacy to talk of the Russian steamroller. There was a simplification about all these new military and despotic States, which only sprang up in the age of mere militarism and mere despotism; in the secular and cynical wars of the eighteenth century. But Austro-Hungary was a thousand things; Austro-Hungary was a thousand years; lapsed kingdoms, feudal fiefs, feudal bishoprics, free cities, abbey lands, scraps of forgotten treaties, remnants of the entanglement of Italy with the Holy Roman Empire. These things had all lived together somehow in a muddle, but not in a murderous discord of the sort that divides the Prussian from the Pole. There was relatively an atmosphere of enlightenment; and the light was very largely at least a reflection of the ancient sunlight of the Mediterranean. The number of Austrians who could at any time be persuaded to take part in some utterly brutal piece of vandalism or violence, was much smaller than the corresponding number of ordinary Germans. That is the meaning of the present stand of Austria against the Nazis; and the world hangs on it; and I wish we had made the support stronger.

Many in our compulsorily educated culture have laughed very loud at a certain buffoon called William Shakespeare, because he talked about a sea-coast of Bohemia. I doubt whether most of them know anything about the land frontier of Bohemia, or are even very certain of what has become of Bohemia. I do not mean that the Empire should have been artificially retained against the nations; only I doubt whether most of the politicians understood the new nations any more than the old Empire. I think it was entirely right to restore the medieval kingdom of Bohemia, which was only destroyed by an almost accidental victory of the Turks. But I have never understood why it should change its name to Czechoslovakia, which is rather like restoring the ancient nationality of Ireland, adding a thin and arbitrary strip of Scotland, and calling it Celtocaledonia. I do not see why Serbs should not be called Serbs, under which name they have sung great epics and fought heroic battles; but only called Southern Slavs, which is about as sensible as calling Irishmen Western Aryans. But I agree that some redistribution of Austro-Hungarian elements was reasonable enough. Hungary was treated with definite injustice, which could quite easily have been avoided. The vital point, however is that all this was done by men who, in the most definite sense, did not know what they were doing. They did not understand that, at its worst, there had always been a vast difference between the Austro-Hungarian compromise and the Prussian or Russian coercion. We ought to have weakened Prussia and

if anything strengthened Austria. We did in fact
weaken Austria and relatively strengthen Prussia.
And at this moment every man in his five wits is
wishing we had done the opposite.

We shall go on making those ghastly blunders,
and paying for them, so long as the ideal of modern
culture is concerned with what is called Progress,
or the Future, or what somebody guesses about
what nobody knows, what will happen the day after
to-morrow; so long as men are accounted cultured
and enlightened if they talk of what will happen next
month, though they are comically ignorant of what
did happen last week; in short, so long as being
enlightened means looking for what will happen
next, and being more blind than the beasts that perish
to everything that has happened already.

IV

PRUSSIA, THE ENEMY OF GERMANY

TO my own simple sceptical mind, there is always something a little odd about writing a history of prehistoric man. But to judge by film and fiction and fashionable expression everywhere, there is no sort of ignorance about the prehistoric. What there really is is ignorance about something else; which I may call the post-historic. I mean that men seem to have no difficulty about going into details about everything that happened before all our chronicles and records began. What they do not know, either in detail or outline, is what happened after the point at which all our chronicles end. All our school history books stop somewhere; and even scientific outlines of universal history must come to an end at last. But there is a great gap between the very last chapter about the very latest events, as they are dealt with in the most up-to-date history, and the very latest news as reported in an up-to-date newspaper. There is a hole in history; a hiatus in the memories of men; and a man who had lost his memory would be rather more misleading if he had only lost

43

it for the last year, or the last year but one, than if he had lost it altogether. Now what strikes me most about modern men, dealing with modern politics, is this. They know what is now happening in the newspapers—even if it is only happening in the newspapers. They also know what did happen in histories; with the charitable assumption that it did also happen in history. But they do not know the facts, or even the falsehoods, about that interval between the end of what is old enough to be history and the beginning of what is new enough to be news.

I propose to note here one example of this neglected interlude, or what I may call for convenience, The Day before Yesterday; especially in connection with those elements of Europe, which are now so terribly near to being elements of explosion. It seems to me that they are mostly miscalculated, not because men read no history, though politicians read precious little history; not because they never read the newspapers, though one really brilliant politician boasted that he never read the newspapers; but because all alike forget this curious class of facts, which are just near enough to be forgotten. I will begin with one of the most menacing facts; I mean all that is involved in talking about Hitler or the Reich or the Rhineland

44

or the frontiers of France—and, above all, the frontiers of Austria.

Now suppose references to " England " were scattered through a review of recent centuries. And suppose we only gradually discovered that the word " England " always referred to what is called " New England ". We should be suddenly enlightened about much that had puzzled us ; as, for instance, why in this account the Roast Beef of Old England served at Christmas had been entirely replaced by turkey and cranberry sauce on Thanksgiving Day ; or why Boston was not in Lincolnshire. Or suppose historians talked of the Archbishop of York ; and we discovered that he was an Episcopalian Methodist who was a bishop in New York. These are extreme parallels perhaps ; but they are not much more extravagant than the error into which every modern person falls when he merely uses the word " Germany ". There certainly is such a place ; but he would be much nearer the truth if he called it " New Germany ". By far the most massive and material fact about it is that it is quite new. As a matter of fact, it is exactly four years older than I am ; and (considered merely as one of the sons of time borne away on its ever-rolling stream) I am quite new. It is newer than New York and much newer than New

The End of the Armistice

England. Of course, there was always Germany in the sense that there were always Germans. But in so far as those Germans had a country, a culture, a common centre of their civilisation, it was never, through all the ages, what we now call Germany. It was what we now call Austria. In so far as they were ruled by a Kaiser, the Emperor of Austria was the one and only Kaiser. In so far as there was a German Empire, the Austrian Empire was the one and only German Empire. They were more loosely federated than the solid nations like France; they could be regarded as small separate kingdoms and dukedoms; but in so far as they were ever one thing, this was the one and only thing. If they belonged to any Empire, it could only conceivably be the Holy Roman Empire, and the great imperial throne upon the Danube.

A small nearly savage state far in the north-east, named Prussia, went Protestant and started picking and stealing and stretching its power against Austria, and to the general disgust of Germany. It produced able adventurers of the predatory Prussian sort, and finally one—Bismarck—who suddenly made war on Austria, and then on France, and in the sensational moment of success, bullied or persuaded his German allies in the north to consent to his own petty Prussian

46

prince being called "the Kaiser" and his particular batch of partisans being called "The German Empire". Nobody had dreamed of such a thing before; and nothing of the sort ever happened till a lifetime ago. It was as if a successful rebellion of Boers, Afrikanders and Outlanders had called itself "The British Empire". That is the real and recent history of the word "Germany".

Now millions of men have heard of the Roman Empire who have never heard of the Holy Roman Empire. Thousands have heard of the Holy Roman Empire who know nothing of its last phase in Austria, parallel with the first phase of Prussia. The Thirty Years War was a Three Hundred Years War, which was not ended when the Protestant hero, Frederick the Great, who had sworn an oath to protect the widowed Empress of Austria, kept it by invading her Empire without even a declaration of war, and robbing her of the whole huge province of Silesia without even the shadow of a justification. It was not ended when the Prussian separatist Bismarck was successful at Sadowa. It was not ended even when his pupils murdered Dollfuss and forbade him the Blessed Sacrament. It will only be ended when the Nazis have annexed and annihilated Austria; the old original Germany. But many

have heard of Dollfuss because he died in the newspapers ; and a few have heard of the Thirty Years
War, because it was contemporary with Cromwell
and Prince Rupert. But if you mention Sadowa or
Silesia to most people, you will find they have forgotten the main modern attack of New Germany on
Old Germany. " Germany " is not like France, an old
Christian nation with anti-Christian revolts. The
whole bunch or bundle of it is only the spoils of an
anti-Catholic raid that had only just happened when
I was born.

V

A PEDANTIC BARBARIAN

IF any one wants to know the truth about Prussia, which we abused for six years and then began suddenly to flatter in the hope of destroying Poland, he will not find it in any of the direct judgments of journalism. During the war, the journalists achieved the rather difficult feat of making out the Prussian culture even worse than it was. Now they are quite in the mood to make it out almost as idiotically sacred and solemn as it professes to be. In both cases their opinions are worthless; if only because, generally speaking, they are not even their opinions. They are written to order to assist some Anti-French or Anti-Polish stunt, as they were written before to assist an Anti-German stunt. If we want a real test, we may find it indeed in the newspapers; but not on the front page and certainly not in the leading article.

What Prussia really is is very precisely recorded in a small newspaper paragraph; which announces that official permission has been given to a large number of earnest thinkers to walk about naked, so long as they preserve certain stated conditions of comparative seclusion. The mad notion of doing such a thing at all, and the tame notion of doing it according to certain police rules—that is Prussia and we might almost say nothing else is Prussia. A curious cold and mechanical discipline covering something utterly unbalanced and barbaric in the soul. This particular instance sounds comic enough ; but let it not be supposed that the actors perceive in it the faintest touch of comedy. There is nothing Rabelaisian about their coarseness ; it is not a joke ; it would be much more Christian and decent if it were. It is utterly, unfathomably, savagely solemn. The Professor is perfectly capable of being spectacles and nothing else ; at any rate he will wear an earnest expression and nothing else. But you could sing to him the dear old English comic song : " And as he'd nothing else to wear, he wore a worried look ", and he would not smile.

It may seem a remarkable reaction from the hundred uniforms of the German Emperor. But that sort of action and reaction are really equal and opposite ; and are part of the same stiff mechanical movement. The Prussian pendulum, like the Prussian sentry, goes to and fro without anything worth calling movement. The worship of blood and iron and the worship of blood and bone are parts of the

same unnatural nature worship. They took the
French ideal of the soldier and spoilt it ; they ran it
to death till the world was sick of the sight of a
uniform. They are quite capable of taking the Greek
ideal of the athlete and translating his Gymnastics
literally till it is the laughing stock of the world. As
they became unsoldierly out of sheer soldiering, so
they will doubtless become even uglier out of pure
love of beauty. For it must not be supposed that
this is a small episode in the nation, corresponding
to the small paragraph in the newspaper. Anybody
who has visited Berlin of late years knows that all
the paper-stalls and book-shops are simply covered
with the propagandist literature of this Adamite
heresy. It is not at all impossible that it may break
yet further out of the red tape that has already been
somewhat loosened around it. We may see another
march of the Adamites as we have seen another
invasion of the Huns. It is not necessary for us, we
imagine, to elaborate the fallacy of this folly. It can
be stated in one sentence. Clothes are natural to
man ; because man is not merely natural. But until
that religion and philosophy is spread to that unfortunate race which still remains barbarous and unbaptised, such lunacies will be let loose on the
world.

VI

THINKING ABOUT EUROPE

THESE are days, we might say hours, we might even be tempted to say minutes, in which everyone who knows anything of Europe knows it to be near to another crack of doom. That is as far as it is necessary to go here in the direction of political detail. But men differ not only about the detail, but about the whole question of the spirit in which such a situation should be met. There are some who are entirely satisfied with demanding what they generally describe as Deeds not Words; and it generally takes them an interminable number of words to say very little in the way of defining the Deeds. There are some who, finding themselves in a desperate difficulty, seem to assume that there can be no remedy except a desperate remedy. They choose the remedy solely because it is desperate; and will not even listen to any counsel unless it is a counsel of despair. These, for instance, will generally be found among the enthusiasts who accept universal Communism; their enthusiasm being tinged with euthanasia; and having a sort of sublime savour of suicide. There are others, at the opposite political extreme, who think that everything can be done still by old men bullying young men by roaring in a raucous voice that all foreigners are fools; or by imagining that they can kick nations as they used to kick niggers. All these various forms of activity, suicide or sweeping destruction, talking very loud about doing something, or threatening something that you cannot possibly do —all these are alike in giving to those indulging in them a deep satisfaction and relaxation of the nerves; a sense that something at least is happening to relieve the strain. But I do not believe in any of them myself; and anyhow the good they do is only personal and psychological. Whatever else may be said for the methods of these practical men, they are not practical.

Nevertheless, I know that few will agree with me about the attitude which I think practical. For I have always thought that thinking is practical; thinking up to the very last moment; thinking in the midst of the battle; thinking when everybody is supposed to be acting; and thinking more calmly, more carefully, and more justly, the more acute becomes the practical crisis. Battles are not won by generals saying, " the time has come for action ", but by generals thinking closely and logically about the wisest way to act. Shipwrecks are not avoided by doing something, but by doing the right thing. Now the great difficulty about doing the right thing, in the relations between England and Europe, lies in the unfortunate fact that the English have hardly ever thought about Europe at all. They have thought about England, which is entirely commendable; they have thought about Empire, which is at least comprehensible; but the notion of having a really rational and objective and well-informed view of the countries of the Continent is very much rarer in this country than some suppose. When the public mood is not mere indifference, it is a rapidly alternating series of likes and dislikes, or what Matthew Arnold truly called hot fits and cold fits; all of them arising from certain hasty impressions about our own advantage or disadvantage; and none of them founded on anything but newspaper stories, which are very often stories in the nursery rather than the newspaper sense. For these reasons I do not apologise for continuing, even at such a crisis, to discuss the European elements in terms which will seem to the practical people very general; and to very vague people will probably appear very vague.

Nor do I believe in dealing with these things in a literal and mechanical and materialistic manner; as some frigid internationalists pride themselves on doing. I do not believe in an equality of labels; or

54

imagining that we can turn Switzerland and Japan and France and Mexico and Turkey and Ireland and China into the same sort of thing, merely by issuing the same sort of tickets to delegates at a Conference. I do not believe in measuring armaments as a speedometer measures miles; without any reference to where the motor-car has gone, or why the motorist went there. The problem is a problem of human will; of human motives and morals, and therefore of human souls. It is the souls of nations that we have, as best we may, to weigh in the balance; to try to be just to them, or even sympathetic with them, but to understand where their spiritual energies diverge from our own; and not to judge them merely by whether they are convenient or inconvenient to our own. It is a difficult thing to do; but the alternative to difficulty is disaster. It requires imagination; that most strenuous and staggering sort of imagination which can see what is really there; where a weaker imagination always sees its own image everywhere.

The first difficulty is that in feeling the true atmosphere of foreign nations it is so easy to fall into the habit of only comparing them unfavourably with our own nation. It will be well before criticising another people, to make it a sort of religious exercise to remember what could be said against our own people. Nearly all of it is connected with a sort of abuse of fancy; a fairyland of play. That is what is meant by saying that we take our play too seriously; we should like to think that it is the whole of life. Other nations amuse themselves; and sometimes, as it seems to us, with amazing futility; as a French merchant will retire from business and seem to do nothing but play dominoes. But he does not mix up his idleness and his ideals. He does not describe a base or caddish action by saying, "It is not dominoes," as the English say, or did till lately say, "It is not cricket." He does not say, "The battle of Austerlitz was won with the dominoes of the *Estaminet Des Apéritifs*" as Wellington said "The battle of Waterloo was won on the playing fields of Eton". On the other hand, he has the faults of his own culture; the faults of a country specially favourable to the peasant and the small shopkeeper. He has his own kind of selfishness, his own kind of materialism, and all the rest. I am English, and I am on the side of the French; but I like to recognise these things first, before attempting to summarise what is really wrong with the other side.

Now it always seems to me that what is wrong with the Germans is hysteria. People may even think this a paradox; because Germans are generally heavy and stodgy, while Italians shout and yell and throw plates. But Italians are not in the least hysterical ; they are only angry. Any doctor will tell you that hysteria is deepest when it is secret and silent ; that is, when it is a sort of permanent sulks. It is a curious sort of sensitiveness and brooding, which breaks out intermittently as bragging. But the brooding and the bragging have both that sort of egoism and self-pity which are almost a medical disease. For some reason or other, the Germans, in many ways so genial and hospitable and human, have encouraged in themselves this deleterious sentimentalism. Whether they lay too long under the shadow of French energy, and developed what is now called an inferiority complex ; or whether it has something to do with their being at their very greatest in the one great art that appeals more directly to the emotions than the reason, music ; or whether it is simply some childish phase of an incomplete civilisation, I do not know. But I am sure the thing is there ; and a permanent fountain of tears and blood ; not always only their own. And, worst of all, to this misfortune is added another, which fits in with it only too well. The Prussian, who is not a German, but some sort of Slav, has somehow managed by sheer insolence to get himself accepted by the simple Germans as a

sort of military mascot; like the goat or other beast
of the field who marches with some regiment in our
own army. The Germans have got it into their
heads that this mascot will always lead them to
victory. They do not seem to be at all affected by
the fact that he last led them to an appalling defeat.
But that is where the secret hysteria comes in. They
cannot bear to call a defeat a defeat, or use it as an
argument even to their own advantage; because it
spoils the secret dream on which such megalo-
maniacs live. When the Prussian gets at the German,
and drugs him with an extra dose of all that produces
this dream, the German becomes something altogether
outside reason. As I said, the labels merely shifted
from one nation to another mean very little. Mussolini
at a crisis may crush all public criticism; but he
knows perfectly well that Italians go on being critical.
But Germans suddenly lose the faculty of criticism;
and above all of self-criticism. They are the ever-
victorious; the emperors of their own imperial
imagination; towering triumphant over all the inconvenient facts of history. One of the greatest of the
Germans, in the days when they had small kingdoms
and great men, wrote the words, " God has given
to the French the land; and to the English the sea;
and to the Germans the clouds ".

PART II
HITLERISM

VII

THE STUPIDEST THING

HAVING been asked the question " What in your opinion were the most stupid things of 1933 ? " I can answer it very simply if I may be permitted to answer it sincerely. By far the stupidest thing done, not only in the last year, but in the last two or three centuries, was the acceptance by the Germans of the Dictatorship of Hitler—to say nothing of Goering. But indeed, it was much worse than that. Any man at any moment may do a stupid thing. It is the rare privilege only of a gifted few to do about six stupid things at once. It is reserved for really fine farcical heroes, like the heroes of the superhuman farces of Mr. P. G. Wodehouse; the sort of stories in which a man lightly throws away a lighted cigar, which at one and the same moment sets fire to his father's most favourable will, spoils his fiancée's beauty, breaks the vase he might have sold for a thousand, sets the hotel on fire involving damages in millions and singes his sister's dog, so that it yelps and bites her wealthy suitor in the leg. That is the sort of grand harmony and unification of comic blunders that the Nazi victory has really achieved. It may be well to enumerate them roughly, as in the case of the far less disastrous gesture of the gentleman with the cigar.

(1) The Germans have silenced the Pro-Germans; without making the slightest difference to the Anti-Germans. Pro-Germans were people found all over the world, but especially in what is called the Anglo-Saxon world; and that not necessarily in any sense that anybody could have counted treasonable during the War. For certain historic, religious or racial causes, which we need not debate, it is true that many a good American or British soldier had more understanding of the Germans he attacked than of the French he defended. I do not feel like that myself; but I am not speaking of feelings but of facts. As a fact, the reaction in favour of Germany had been mixed up with a reaction in favour of Peace. All that worldwide backing has been lost; meanwhile every Pole and every Frenchman is as vigilantly hostile as ever.

(2) It killed the discussion of Disarmament by a new discussion of Rearmament. But again, it was worse still. If a man in a street recently swept by gun-fights puts a cannon on his roof, puts on a new uniform and practises with a pistol in the garden,

The Stupidest Thing

teaches his two sons to hack each other with sabres and flies a flag with a warlike motto, it is rather worse if he then looks over the wall and explains (like Hitler) that he does not mean to fight. Simple people will answer : " You are either a lunatic or a liar, who does intend to fight. The most respectful view is that you are a liar. The only other is one rather worse than both ; that you are a bloody-minded fool who loves to talk and think about fighting, and who dare not fight."

(3) It gained all the ill-fame of fanaticism and yet it was a compromise. It fell between two stools. It might really have won Catholic Germany by dropping a few fads ; which are to Catholics crimes.

(4) The stupidest thing on earth is to destroy your own victory. Again and again they have produced a good effect, and then deliberately made it bad and ineffective. When the German Court acquitted the men accused of burning the Reichstag, a wave went through the world of relief and almost of apology. We all felt that the German judiciary at least was still part of civilisation, remembering justice and the Roman Law. Then they stopped the whole reaction in their favour by carrying out the sentence in flat contradiction of the verdict, and imprisoning men who were acquitted exactly as if they had been con-

demned. They also allowed a crazy bully, named Goering, to howl threats of private and lawless vengeance on the prisoners " if he got them outside ".

(5) Where on earth did he pick up the Swastika ? Has he been living with Red Indians ; and are they Aryans ? The thing has cut him off from all the serious culture of the world. The Swastika is most famous as an Asiatic symbol. But what does it symbolise ? It is rather a good symbol and speaks for itself. It means Recurrence ; the recognition of sameness ; all that is meant by the Wheel of Buddha. In short, it means the opposite of all that is meant by the Nazi Revolution. They have brandished it ; blazoned it ; done everything except look at it. Whatever the Nazis want, they do not want to look like Hindoos.

(6) They have done the one thing which is the mark of the eternal or temporary Fool. We all tend to do it, because we all occasionally tend to be fools. But historically it is fatal. They have only answered their accusers by praising themselves.

VIII

THE TRIBAL TRIUMPH[1]

ANYONE old enough to remember even faintly the last days of Queen Victoria, and the gradual change in international information which had appeared even before the Great War, will be astounded at two things about the tribal triumph now parading among the Germans. The first staggering fact is the fact that a fresh generation can boil up again, in so frothy a fuss, over anything so utterly stale. The second staggering fact is that a whole huge people should base its whole historical tradition on something that is not so much a legend as a lie. A legend is something that grows slowly and naturally and generally does symbolise some sort of relative truth about history. The legend of Arthur is legendary in this sense; but it does symbolise the enormous and once neglected truth, that if Britain had not once had a Roman basis, it would never have had any basis at all. But the myth of the modern Germans, especially in its relation to the ancient Germans, was made quite recently

[1] This essay was written as an Introduction to a pamphlet containing a selection of Nazi writings, edited by Lord Tyrrell.

and quite artificially; it was invented by professors and imposed by schoolmasters; and it has not even the remotest connection with any historical truth whatever.

The first fact, the strange staleness which makes the racial religion stink in our nostrils with the odours of decay, and of something dug up when it was dead and buried, need not principally concern us. A man who has revelled in Carlyle as a boy, reacted against him as a man, re-reacted with saner appreciation as an older man, and ended, he will hope, by seeing Carlyle more or less where he really stands, can only be amazed at this sudden reappearance of all that was bad and barbarous and stupid and ignorant in Carlyle, without a touch of what was really quaint and humorous in him. The real Carlyle, who was a Scotchman and therefore understood a joke, has been entirely replaced by the theoretical Carlyle, who was a Prussian and not allowed to see a joke. And he seems never to have seen the joke of the great Teutonic Theory, which he handed on to Kingsley and in a less degree to Freeman and Froude; and which was in my childhood the fashionable fad in English as well as German education. That all this nonsense of the nursery should suddenly start up like a spectre in my path, in my normal journey towards the grave, strikes me as something quite incredible. It is as incredible as seeing Prince Albert come down from the Albert Memorial and walk across Kensington Gardens. But it is specially incredible because, since that day, the historical theory which Froude and Freeman and others shared with Carlyle, the theory of a Teutonic root of all the real greatness of Europe, has been criticised by saner historians, with a broader outlook which the Victorians never imagined, and often with a number of new facts which the Victorians could not be expected to know. To-day, no well-informed person has any right to be ignorant of the part really played, not by the Germanic chaos, but by the Roman order and the Catholic faith, in the making of everything civilised or half-civilised, including Germany.

In the light of this elementary degree of education, examine some of the statements lately made by the most popular and enthusiastic Nazi writers—passing over for the moment the cases of flat contradiction, where the Nordic notion contradicts not only every Christian virtue but every common human generosity, as in saying that " the conception of Christian charity causes national degeneration inasmuch as it involves caring for the physically weak and infirm." Let us take first the virtues on which the Christian and the Nordic man would agree ; though the Nordic man has the cheek to claim them as his alone. Take

The End of the Armistice

the ridiculous statement, repeated again and again; the notion that there is something specially German about "the idea of honour". There is not the faintest historical truth, or even historical meaning, in this claim. Imagine the Prussian professor slowly and carefully reading Horace's version of the story of Regulus and duly noting down the fact that no Latins or men of the Mediterranean have had any idea of honour. One would suppose that anybody could see the absurdity of that; that everybody can, in a general way, trace the conception of keeping faith, refusing cowardly comfort or safety, feeling surrender as a stain, through all the great story of antiquity, through the Pagan philosophers defying tyrants, through the Christian martyrs accepting torments, through the Christian knights and paladins careful to keep the vow, or fulfil the conditions of the quest. To call it a German idea is about as sensible as to call it a Finnish idea or an Icelandic idea. Since all men, even the rudest, have some rude form of conscience, it did doubtless exist more or less in various Teutons, as in various Celts and Slavs and Semitic Arabs. But the most powerful examples of it, the clearest praises of it, the longest tradition of it, descend to us all down that long Roman road which connects ancient with modern civilisation.

The Tribal Triumph

In these few lines I have confined myself to the
Nazi literature, which is on the face of it opposed
to common sense and common historical information and is in conflict with the Catholic conscience
and the principal religious authority of Europe. It
is worth while to note how much the two elements
of normal instincts and of supernatural doctrine are
at this moment in agreement. Rome stands just
now not only for reason, but rather especially for
common sense; and, as in this case, for common
justice to the common people. It is this influence
which the Nazi writers describe as so subtle a social
poison; the southern influence which, creeping north
into the virgin forests, corrupted the simple Germans
with the habit of building houses, of making roads, of
riding horses, of talking in an intelligible, or more or
less intelligible manner. For those great gods, the early
Germans of the forests, to whom all " creative " energy
is due, did not of themselves set up one building that
has remained, or carve one statue of even prehistoric
value, or express in any shrine or symbol the confused
mythology which some would substitute for the
radiant lucidity of the Faith. The great German civilisation was created by the great Christian civilisation;
and its heathen forerunners left it nothing whatever;
except an intermittent weakness for boasting.

IX

WHO IS DICTATOR?

IT has been urged that Hitler's raving appeals to racial pride and hatred and (what is worse) contempt, were assumed entirely out of policy in order to ensure popularity. All the time, he had within the tranquil glow of an ideal of international friendship, and felt nothing but the charity and humility of a true Catholic towards his fellow-Catholics and his fellow-creatures. Thus, when he told the Germans that their outlet was choked by " the lousy Poles ", it was merely for convenience that he chose this form of expressing his affection for Poland ; and when he indicated, in the same sentence, the well-known fact that Frenchmen are Negroes, and (worse still) are afflicted with Militarism, he did but dissemble his love in the manner of Hamlet, by wilfully pretending to be insane. Perhaps the last accusation, by the way, is the most interesting of all. Blackness is a matter of taste ; the Ethiopian visages of Foch and Poincaré and Maurras and Maritain rise before our memories with varied effect according to our moods. But to think that any nation should defile itself by Militarism !

70

Who is Dictator?

To suppose that any Prussian Imperialist or German patriot could be expected to pardon that !

Now I do not mean to sneer when I say that it is really rather a difficult business to recast one's opinions of a man, on the avowed principle that he meant the opposite of what he said. But there is another difficulty raised by this theory; and it is really my own difficulty in the whole matter. It might be expressed by saying that it is not merely the question of whether Hitler is entirely Prussianist, but of whether the new Prussianism is entirely Hitler. For on this point we must follow the argument carefully. In effect, it is this : that Prussianism in Prussia was so strong, so stiff, so rooted, so ineradicable and incurable, that any man hoping to have any hearing was forced to begin by flattering it. He was coerced into talking nonsense about lousy foreigners, because if he had dared to say a word of Christian common sense, the Prussian pride and prejudice would have been strong enough to crush and silence him. Now this may or may not be true ; but if it is true, it raises another serious question. If the old narrow Prussianism was as strong as that a few months ago, is it not possible that it is as strong as that still ? If the Catholic and humane Hitler was forced to obey it then, is it not possible that he will be forced to obey it now? And though he himself may have abused the Poles without any desire to attack the Poles, may not the most militaristic gang in Europe, the old guard of the Junkers, determine on their own account to attack Poland, and over-rule the remonstrances of Hitler by quotations from the eloquent and moving speeches in which he had himself abused Poland? In other words, the question is, even if Germany is a Dictatorship, who is really the Dictator? And surely we may be allowed to doubt whether the Dictator must of necessity be the same man whom his own admirers and defenders excuse as having talked entirely at the dictation of somebody else. A Dictator may be all sorts of things, good or bad. But a Dictator is not dictated to; and, by this version of his story, Hitler was dictated to.

In short, the difficulty is that the powers and influences are indeterminate; and that is in another way the difficulty of the whole German problem; and what makes the Hitlerite problem different, for instance, from the Fascist problem. Hitler has not risen to power by enunciating a certain theory of the State; certainly not by any of the very excellent later experiments, in which he has shown the increasing influence of the Distributist State. He has admittedly risen by appealing to racial pride; and the racial pride of the Germans really is a rather peculiar thing, and different from normal patriotism or even Jingoism. Its frontiers, for instance, are curiously vague and shifting. Hitler's apologists ask why a man should not desire to restore order in his own country. But Hitler did not restore order in his own country. He went to what would normally be called a foreign country, except that it was linked up by some loose theories about Aryans and Teutons and the heathen worshippers of the Swastika. In this sort of anthropological atmosphere, what is his own country ? Where *is* the German's Fatherland ? Or rather, where is it not ?

If it happened to be convenient to Hitler to annex two English counties, as it was convenient to Moltke to annex two French provinces, he could annex Norfolk and Suffolk without calling a blush of Aryan blood to his cheek. Are they not the North Folk and the South Folk ? Are not their very names in the true-hearted German folk-speech spoken ? If ever that situation arose, it would be quite useless for you and me to say that Nelson was a Norfolk man, and that it is infernal nonsense to say that Nelson was a German. A hundred professors would leap up to explain that Nelson was true, valiant, a Viking, a sea-saga's-hero, and therefore obviously

The End of the Armistice

was a German. . . . Do you think that is fantastic? It is not one shade more fantastic than, it is indeed identical with, the claim actually made by Germans to the whole province of Lorraine. I have seen long and learned German arguments, showing that Joan of Arc was a German; because she was brave and true and pious and lived in Lorraine. A young woman lives and dies to crown the French King in the French shrine, fights under the French oriflamme to clear the French soil of foreigners; and the German professors say she was a German. The German soldiers agree with the German professors; or rather the German professors agree with the German soldiers. The German soldiers ruled for fifty years in Lorraine and they may yet land in Norfolk. That is the sort of thing I am troubled about; not the precise balance of the theories of Dictatorship and Distributism in the mind of one man, who has admittedly expressed all sorts of other ideas in an entirely unbalanced manner. I can quite believe that Hitler has his good points; I know that he has his good policies. But if he has disguised his policies out of policy, who dictated that policy? I want to know whether the old Prussia is still leading the Germanies. If she is, I know that she will lead them into war.

X

IF IT WERE ENGLAND

I HAVE been revolving the point of conscience (part of the defence of Hitler referred to in the previous essay), about what I should do, if I wished to dominate and transform my country in a rapid manner; whether I should do what Herr Hitler has done; whether I should say what Herr Hitler has said; and whether I should accept the somewhat alarmingly useful theory that what he said may be completely disconnected from what he thought. But I have honestly tried to test the matter in the only imaginative, and, therefore, the only practical way, by taking the case of my own country; to which, oddly enough, I happen to be attached. I am an Englishman; and I think I am almost as fond of England as an Austrian can be of Prussia. At the same time, I cannot be answered by any charges of merely pitting my own patriotism against that of the foreigner. In so far as patriotism has a parody that is called Jingoism, I have condemned it in my own country quite as much as in any other. I have always been opposed to British Imperialism; ever since my first journalistic efforts defended the Boers against the blind unanimity and brutal optimism of the first phase of the South African War. But neither, on the other side, do I admit that such Imperialism is too preposterous to support, on the same grounds on which a German may support German Imperialism. The parallel I make is not equal or exact; and leaves my argument an argument *a fortiori*. When all is said and done, if I could not conscientiously profess British Imperialism, still less could I profess Prussian Imperialism.

I know it is the custom to equalise all these things, and talk of the pot calling the kettle black. I will not insist on the abstract logical truth; that a truthful pot has a perfect right to confess its own blackness and still call the kettle black. In my own case, I will only say that a man who has tried for thirty years to clean the pot certainly has the right to call the kettle black, when it is really blacker than the pot. And it is blacker than the pot. I know all about English insolence, in some Irish or other relations; but if anybody says it is the same as Prussian insolence, I say it is not. I said so when Mr. Bernard Shaw advanced the parallel in the first days of the War. He said that Prussian Junkers were no worse than English aristocrats and officers in the Guards. Now

If It Were England

it is a fact attested by solid evidence, that Prussian officers used to elbow ladies off the pavement and practically kick them into the gutter. I entirely agree that an English officer may be an insolent noodle, with a narrow contempt for everybody else and a class-arrogance that cries to God for vengeance. But he does not elbow ladies into the gutter. And that cold concrete fact does mean a total difference between two types and two cultures.

Therefore, the parallel case offered me ought to be an easy one. I ought to find it more tolerable to flatter the Jingoism of English people, than I should if they were Prussian people. I do in fact find them and all their sentiments and stupidities more tolerable than those of Prussian people. But, even so, am I to picture myself as doing in England exactly what Hitler is represented (by his own champions) as doing in Germany? How am I to obtain that despotic power, which I shall wield so drastically and yet so justly for the purge of morals and the restoration of unity, if this is to be done by appealing to anything in England that may happen to be quite as nonsensical as the Nordic Race, and about as tenth-rate as the Swastika? Is that the way it should be done; and am I to appeal to the fools of England by a corresponding frenzy of folly?

The End of the Armistice

Behold me setting forth on my political mission, wearing the Old Boys' Tie, or the Guards' Tie, or some gentlemanly combination of the two; and making my first speech; about how we English understand how to Play the Game while the negroid Irish and the lousy French cannot understand that Cricket is Character and Character is Cricket. Listen to the ringing peroration, in which I describe how Beit and Rhodes did but continue the chivalrous dash of Wolfe and Nelson; and how every British Business Man, when he Delivers the Goods, feels something within him of that which steered the Victory and stormed the Heights of Abraham. Moving in my triumphant political progress, from Cheltenham to Bath, and from Bath to Clifton, I electrify a thousand old ladies of the Tory Party by telling them that what they want is a Strong Man, and that I mean to shoot down the damned strikers and put Ireland under martial law to-morrow. Confronted with Socialists or Communists, in any public debate, I let fall those wise and pulverising words, that used to fall so weightily from the lips of my dear great-uncle Humphrey, in the days of Queen Victoria : " If you were to divide it all up to-morrow it would all be back in the same hands " ; or alternatively, " Now you want to make everybody equal, but nature hasn't made us all equal"; with the logical inference that nature has made me worth £5,000 and the nearest clever chauffeur or engineer worth £1 a week. Yes . . . yes . . . I must say all that; I must go through with it. By hypothesis, of course, I do not believe a word of it; but I am appealing to the old patriotic traditions of my country, in order to gain the power to save her in her peril. Literal translators are the worst liars; and they often say that it is sweet and decorous to die for our country. Being liars, they may perhaps also say that it is sweet and decorous to lie for our country. And so, in order to seize the Dictatorship of the Distributist State, I must do what Hitler has done, to seize the Dictatorship of the Hitlerite State. When once I am Dictator, I can turn round on them all and tell them what fools they were to believe a word I said. It is a necessary way of achieving popularity.

But must I really crawl on my stomach like that through all the foulest filth of the world? And is there not after all a case against such cynicism, even from the cynical point of view? If I flatter all that is most false in England, shall I find an England ready and eager to listen to all that is most painful and most true?

XI

THE DEATH OF DOLLFUSS

ABOUT ten days ago the Nazis killed the Austrian Chancellor; and, while they were about it, quite probably killed the Nazi movement. That stupendous stupidity, which always seems to me the chief character of the Third Reich, and which is commonly the penalty of any worship of Pride, led them into a characteristic contradiction between their tyranny and their anarchy. There is much that can be said, and from the dawn of history has been said, for and against suppression and for and against self-expression. It is typical of the Nazis that they try to suppress everything unfavourable to them, and then walk out wantonly and do the things that cannot be suppressed. They have a queer dull faith in the accomplished fact; even when it has accomplished a totally different fact. Herr Dollfuss is undoubtedly dead and buried; and Herr Hitler is undoubtedly walking about solid in the sunlight. It is typical of him that his government explained the death of several perfectly well-known Catholic popular leaders, by saying they had committed suicide. These people do

The Death of Dollfuss

not know the difference between a statement that may quiet a storm of enquiry, and a statement that is certain to raise one. I wonder Herr Hitler does not say that Herr Dollfuss committed suicide. It is quite certain, in the larger social and spiritual sense, that neither Catholics nor Catholicism, either in Germany or in Austria, has the slightest reason or even temptation to commit suicide. But there may be some truth in the rumour that Hitler has committed suicide.

It is quite likely that the murder of Dollfuss may swing the whole world round again ; as did, for instance, the murder of St. Thomas of Canterbury. Before Thomas Becket was murdered, a very large number of Catholics, of clerics, of leading ecclesiastics, were inclined to regard him as an extravagant nuisance. Many good Catholics had opposed Becket ; and many good Catholics have supported Hitler. But St. Thomas dead was ten times stronger than St. Thomas alive. The backwash of popular indignation was so overpowering, that a great king was beaten with rods before his own subjects. But our manners have grown more polished and humane ; and we should be more horrified by the idea of a successful public man being hit with a stick, than by the comparatively casual occurrence of his being shot dead with a pistol. It was really part of the case for St. Thomas of Canterbury that the minor punishments of the Church were on the whole milder than the minor punishments of the State. But in these emancipated days we have passed even beyond the idea of definite secular punishment, and escaped into a freer world of irresponsible and opportunist assassination. The death of Dollfuss, as distinct from the life of Dollfuss, carries with it this primary and preliminary lesson; that this sort of highly practical politics is not even practical. Whatever else is true, it is most emphatically not true that dead men tell no tales. They have told nearly all the tales, upon which both legend and history have arisen.

The tale which Dollfuss dead will live to tell is very much larger than the life of Dollfuss living; in the common literary sense which identifies a life with a biography. He tells the tale of ten or twelve centuries; and all that has happened since Rome became a reality for the southern Germanies, and especially for the people of the Danube, while it was still only a rumour, or at best a romance, for the more northern tribes. He stood for the fact that Germans were not barbarians, that they had been baptised and civilised, and that for centuries their centre was Vienna. To the north and east of them

82

there lay a race of men who have always had the
simple, single and unchanging object of proving that
the Germans are not civilised and not Christian.
And, to do them justice, it must be admitted that
during the last few centuries they have been rather
successful in proving their thesis. Prussia set out
to prove the theory that Germans are by nature
barbarians. Of course a number of other words were
actually used; that the Germanic spirit was free
from Judaic and Papist influences; that the German
blood guaranteed an emancipation from Latin and
Semitic superstitions; and so on. But what it meant
was that Teutons like to be barbaric and are going
to be as barbaric as they like. Against this slander
upon a European race there stood up one permanently standing contradiction; and its name was
Austria. Everybody knew that Vienna was a place
of culture and tradition, like Paris and like Rome.
The thought that any Germans anywhere could have
condescended to common courtesy, to humanity, nay
(more horrible still) to humility, filled the half-
heathen Teutons of the north with that sort of
furious and hungry hatred, with which the inferior
always regards the superior. The Nazi movement
in Austria was quite simply a movement to barbarise
Austria; to unbaptise Austria.

The End of the Armistice

Against this heathen horde Engelbert Dollfuss, a small man of poor and peasant ancestry, stood up by the ancient instinct of such ancestry, resolved to save the remnant of the Roman civilisation of Germany. That is his historical importance; and it is probable that by being murdered he has saved it. It is a secondary matter to sum up the rest of his career, which, like any other career, contains any number of things about which any number of people will very naturally debate and differ. He was faced at one time by that most horrible experience which any patriot can suffer; that which Macaulay truly called, "that last and most dreadful extreme of faction rage; that last and most cruel test of military fidelity". Of the suppression of the Socialist rising (by those whom our newspapers insist on calling the Fascist Party, but who were simply the Peasant Party) I will say only this. That any judgment on it is worthless, which does not face the fundamental fact; that it was dealing with Mutiny in time of War. It is obvious but inadequate to say that Dollfuss was fighting upon two fronts. He was an Austrian patriot, a Catholic very considerate of the claims of the proletariat, who found himself attacked from behind by the Communists, at the very moment when he was defending his own country against tyrants who had oppressed everybody, including the Communists. I have been all my life on the side of the Trades Unions. I have been all my life on the side of the Irish. But suppose I had held the lonely responsibility, at a moment when they revolted, when England was nearly extinguished, as Austria was nearly extinguished. God alone knows what any of us would have done.

But for this one episode, which has been widely and not unnaturally criticised, the life of Dollfuss was not only simple, but was rather dedicated to the ideals of simplicity. He entered politics representing what is now a commonplace in Europe, but still quaintly rather a paradox in England : the identity of Catholic Action with popular reform ; the Christian Social Movement. All his life he was politically as well as personally a peasant. Just as he came first from a farm which his own family is still working as a farm, so he emerged even in his legislative life as an expert on agriculture and a partisan of the peasant parties. Almost all the comments of our national journalism, even at its best, are necessarily inadequate upon that point. In our country talking about a Peasant is rather like talking about a Pirate. Some individuals may idealise a Peasant ; as admirers of Sir Francis Drake would idealise a Pirate. Some may merely despise a Peasant ; as those who hung in chains the later and less fortunate followers of the profession presumably despised a Pirate. But none of us has ever *seen* a Pirate ; and none of us, in this our island home, has ever seen a Peasant. That sort of civilisation could never be destroyed in England ; for the simple reason that, by the opinion of the expert, it cannot be created in England. But that was the sort of civilisation for which Dollfuss died ; and it is quite likely that his death will become a legend. Nothing would be more typical of the traditions from remote times, than the tale of a dwarf who led armies that defeated the stupid giants of the German forests. But whether or no he will be remembered on earth will matter to him very little ; for though the swine who trod over him forbad him even a priest, we know upon what Name he called when he died.

XII

THE OTHER CHEEK

THERE is one funny thing about the relations of Hitler, or at least of Hitlerism, with the New German Protestant Church; or what may be respectfully called the Reformation of the Reformation. It is solidly asserted in several reputable organs that one of the reforms of the new regime will be the complete rejection of the Old Testament. And this puzzles me a good deal, as I gaze at the actual record and activities of Adolf the Aryan. If he had wanted to cut out the New Testament, I could understand it. But, putting aside for the moment all our own convictions on religious matters (and my own involve the acceptation of both the Old Testament and the New as having a sacred origin), there is a sense in which all reasonable people would agree that both these great religious records contain things that may strike an outsider as extreme, or perplexing. They contain what we should call mysteries, but what a heathen might be excused for calling paradoxes. But the curious thing is (and that is itself perhaps one of the mysteries or paradoxes) that the two

sometimes seem to be at opposite extremes; and
that the difficulties of the one are almost opposite
to the difficulties of the other. Now I should have
thought that the counsels of perfection in the New
Testament would be what would stick in the throat
of a Nazi; and not the toleration of imperfection in
the Old Testament; of an imperfection which need
hardly trouble a Nazi at all. Some critics of the
Bible have complained of the tribal ferocity and
violence of Joshua and Jephthah smiting the Can-
aanites; but surely that would all come very natural
to a Nordic Man. Other critics of the Bible have
complained of the utter meekness and self-effacing
non-resistance of some moral ideals in the Sermon
on the Mount. But surely meekness and self-effacing
non-resistance is not what is the matter with poor
Hitler.

Yet it seems that I must be wrong, if the newspapers
are right about the Hitlerite support for this dis-
crimination between the Two Covenants. The New
Testament tells Hitler to turn the other cheek; and
Hitler can do that quite easily. It tells him to love
all his enemies, all the Jews and Socialists, all the
lousy Poles and negroid Frenchmen; and he finds
that as easy as falling off a log. It tells him to give
to a robber even more than the robber has taken;

to remove his waistcoat and hand it to a Jew who has just stolen his coat. Or, to take a more topical example in practical politics, if he really does think that the Poles have stolen Poznan, he will naturally make them a further present of Pomerania. If it be true that the French have wrongly retaken Strasbourg, what more easy for Hitler, in his evangelical ardour for the New Testament ideal, than to present them with some other little trifle like Nuremberg or Cologne? I am well aware that this is not the normal or necessary interpretation of the Christian Counsels of Perfection, in relation to any normal Christian. But we are not dealing with a normal Christian ; but by hypothesis with one who recoils in horror from the primitive epic of the Hebrew heroes, which most Christians can understand and accept ; and who is therefore presumably of an exquisite and intense sensibility about the wickedness of such wars and the corresponding necessity of the New Testament ideals of peace. It must mean that he is specially repelled by the part of the Bible that deals in the extremes of feud and fighting ; but not re-pelled at all by the part of the Bible that deals in equally extraordinary extremes of forgiveness and peace among men. And then I look at the way in which the Hitlerites, or most of the German Protestants for that matter, have been going on lately, and once more I am perplexed ; I cannot make it out at all.

I cannot, as I say, understand why the Nazi should particularly dislike the Old Testament, unless it is because it is full of Jews. So, for that matter, is the New Testament. But it seems strange that the Nazis cannot forgive in prehistoric nomads, fighting for their lives in a desert, the sort of violence which they themselves have brought back into the modern world, and encouraged in clerks and shopkeepers suddenly starting to murder each other in a civilized city. Whatever even a hostile critic might think about The Sword of the Lord and of Gideon, it hardly seems as if Hitler had instantly obeyed that later command of the Lord (to which he is so devoutly attached) which ordered the smiter to put up his sword in the sheath. I do not accept the doctrine of the Quakers any more than the Hitlerites ; but neither do I knock my fellow-townsmen about in the streets and then abolish the Book of Kings because it is full of fighting. This little logical knot, or entanglement between Evangelicanism and Imperialism and Modernism, in the extraordinary German mind, has, however, a certain connection with other considerations, to which this presentation of the problem must in some sense serve as an introduction.

The Other Cheek

The problem can only be solved by considering the very amazing and even monstrous history of Protestantism and Modernism in modern Germany; but that history is of considerable interest and importance, not merely in relation to religion, but in relation to politics; and especially to the painfully practical politics which Germany and Europe at present suffer. The problem, as I have stated it, makes no sense. That is why I have stated it. That is why, of course, it is the form in which the newspapers have stated it. In order to make any sense, it is necessary to face the fact of a rather remarkable sort of nonsense; about which I hope to say something more fully in the next article.

XIII

THE JUDAISM OF HITLER

HITLERISM is almost entirely of Jewish origin.
This truth, if inscribed in the noble old German
lettering on a large banner and lifted in sight of an
excited mob in a modern German town, might or
might not have the soothing effect which I desire.
This simple historical explanation, if written on a
post-card or a telegraph-form, and addressed to Herr
Hitler's private address, might or might not cause
him to pause in his political career, and reconsider
all human history in the light of the blazing illumina-
tion with which I have furnished him in these words.
Finally, these words, placed even where they stand
at the beginning of this paragraph, may not be wholly
comprehended or connected with their true historical
origins ; but they are none the less strictly historical.

It is a horrible shame to say I was ever unkind
to a Nordic Man. I have had many of these innocent
creatures of God gambolling round my house from
time to time, and I have always found them faithful
and affectionate ; when treated and trusted, as they
should be, with faith and affection. I am very fond

of the real Nordic Man, especially when he does really look like a Nordic Man ; as, for example, when he is a Scandinavian. I think the Scandinavian is a thoroughly nice fellow; and probably a much better man than I. Hitler does not look in the least like a Nordic Man ; but that is another question, and need not discredit his personal good qualities. But, when it comes to the reading of history, there is one thing that I can never for the life of me see. I can easily believe that a nice large Scandinavian may have brought great elements of strength or simplicity into any family into which he married ; and what is true of the Scandinavian may be quite often true of the German. But what I frankly and flatly deny, in history as a whole, is that Nordic Men have excelled in bringing *ideas* into the world. The Germans came in due course to describe their piracy as imperialism ; but they borrowed the idea of imperialism from the Romans. They produced a sort of Prussianism that was praised or blamed as militarism ; but they borrowed the idea of militarism from the French. The German Emperors modelled themselves on the Austrian Emperors, who had modelled themselves on the Greek Emperors and the Roman Emperors. The greatest of the Prussians did not even conceal his contempt for Prussia. He

refused to talk anything but French, or to exchange
ideas with anybody, except somebody of the type
of Voltaire. Then came the liberal ideas of the
French Revolution, and the whole movement of
German Unity was originally a liberal movement
on the lines of the French Revolution. Then came
the more modern and much more mortally dangerous
idea of Race, which the Germans borrowed from a
Frenchman named Gobineau. And on top of that
idea of Race, came the grand, imperial idea of a Chosen
Race, of a sacred seed that is, as the Kaiser said, the
salt of the earth; of a people that is God's favourite
and guided by Him, in a sense in which He does not
guide other and lesser peoples. And if anybody asks
where anybody got *that* idea, there is only one
possible or conceivable answer. He got it from the
Jews.

It is perfectly true that the Jews have been very
powerful in Germany. It is only just to Hitler to
say that they have been too powerful in Germany.
But the Germans will find it very hard to cut up their
culture on a principle of Anti-Semite amputation.
They will find it difficult to persuade any German,
let alone any European who is fond of Germany,
that Schiller is a poet and Heine is not; that Goethe
is a critic and Lessing is not; that Beethoven is a

composer and Mendelssohn is not; or that Bach is a musician and Brahms is not. But again, it is but just to Hitlerism to say that the Jews did infect Germany with a good many things less harmless than the lyrics of Heine or the melodies of Mendelssohn. It is true that many Jews toiled at that obscure conspiracy against Christendom, which some of them can never abandon; and sometimes it was marked not by obscurity but obscenity. It is true that they were financiers, or in other words usurers; it is true that they fattened on the worst forms of Capitalism; and it is inevitable that, on losing these advantages of Capitalism, they naturally took refuge in its other form, which is Communism. For both Capitalism and Communism rest on the same idea: a centralisation of wealth which destroys private property. But among the thousand and one ways in which Semitism affected Germanism is in this mystical idea, which came through Protestantism. Here the Nordic Men, who are never thinkers, were entirely at the mercy of the Jews, who are always thinkers. When the Reformation had rent away the more Nordic sort of German from the old idea of human fellowship in a Faith open to all, they obviously needed some other idea that would at least look equally large and towering and transcendental. They began to get it through

95

the passionate devotion of historical Protestants to
the Old Testament. That, of course, is where the
joke comes in; that the Protestants now wish to
select for destruction what nobody else except the
Protestants had ever wanted to select and set apart
for idolatry. But that is a later stage of the story.
By concentrating on the ancient story of the Covenant
with Israel, and losing the counterweight of the idea
of the universal Church of Christendom, they grew
more and more into the mood of seeing their religion
as a mystical religion of Race. And then, by the same
modern processes, their education fell into the hands
of the Jews. There are Jewish mystics and Jewish
sceptics; but about this one matter of the strange
sacredness of his own race, almost every Jewish
sceptic is a Jewish mystic. When they insinuated
their ideals into German culture, they doubtless very
often acted, not only as sceptics, but as cynics. But,
even if they were only pretending to be mystics,
they could only pretend to understand one kind of
mysticism. Thus, German mysticism became more
and more like Jewish mysticism: a thing not thinking
much of ordinary human beings, the hewers of wood
and drawers of water, the Gentiles or the strangers;
but thinking with intense imagination of the idea of
a holy house or family, alone dedicated to heaven and

therefore to triumph. This is the great Prussian illusion of pride, for which thousands of Jews have recently been rabbled or ruined or driven from their homes. I am certainly not enough of an Anti-Semite to say that it served them right.

But it is true that it all began with the power of the Jews ; which has now ended with the persecution of the Jews. People like the Hitlerites never had any ideas of their own ; they got *this* idea indirectly through the Protestants, that is primarily through the Prussians, but they got it originally from the Jews. In the Jews it has even a certain tragic grandeur ; as of men separated and sealed and waiting for a unique destiny. But until we have utterly destroyed it among Christians, we shall never restore Christendom.

XIV

THE HERESY OF RACE

I AM not a fool who fancies the line between the Allies and the Central Powers was a division between angels and devils. I do not even say it was a division between Christians and heathens, still less between Catholics and Protestants. But I do say that it was a division between Catholicism and Prussianism, which is the particular sort of heathenism to which Protestantism has degenerated in certain places. Of course there are millions of Protestants to whom the description of that degeneration does not apply; just as there are millions of magnificent Catholics in the Prussianised Empire to whose general policy it does apply. Nevertheless, it was the old Catholic morality, even if applied by atheists, even if assumed by hypocrites, against a new heathen morality; which was the whole force on the Prussian side. That is my thesis.

I have already shown that the real Outline of History for the last few centuries largely consisted of Prussia dragging down the Holy Roman Empire, and transferring the Imperial Crown, the Kaiserdom

The Heresy of Race

or Kingship of the Germanies, from the old Catholic
Princes who claimed to have it from Charlemagne,
to a Protestant prince who had been but lately a
Prussian squire. In short, the whole modern business
has been the building up of a new Protestant Empire
in the north, on the ruin of the old Catholic Empire
in the south. In this article I would pass from the
test of history to the test of philosophy. I think it
can be shown that the ground on which the Allies
stood was the old ground of Christendom; that of
their enemies a new ground of Anti-Christian and,
as we say, anarchic notions. Both the historic and
philosophic truth can be clearly seen in the one com-
pact case of Alsace-Lorraine. First, historically
speaking, France claimed it on the old assumption
of the settled frontiers of international law, claiming
that the foe had stolen it by violence. In so far as
the Reich made any historical claim, what was it?
It was very interesting. Alsace-Lorraine had never
in any earthly sense belonged to the northern Reich.
There was none to belong to. Centuries ago, it had
once consisted of feudal bishoprics, remotely and
nominally subordinate to the Holy Roman Empire.
If it had ever belonged to anybody, except France,
it must have belonged to Austria. Why was it not
to be restored to Austria? Why, for the very simple

reason I have stated. That Austria was bankrupt, by the Prussian theory; that Prussia had succeeded to all her debts or credits; that, though the Holy Roman Empire was once ' Germany ', it was dead and the Reich was now ' Germany '. In taking Alsace-Lorraine, Prussia robbed Austria if she did not rob France. She robbed her of all her claims as the old suzerain of the Germans. So much for history; but the fact is far clearer when we come to the world of ideas.

What is mostly missed is this fact. The French and Germans not only differ about who has a right to Alsace, but they differ about what is meant by having a right to it. They have not only conflicting claims, but contradictory tests. And the reason is this; that in the lands of the new religions, rapidly turning into new irreligions, there had already sprung up a number of new tests and theories; of which the most menacing was the new theory of Race. The word Nation can be used in either sense. Nationalism, as commonly used now by Catholics condemning the excess of it, means that my nation has a claim to all my worship, and no other nations have claims to anything. Naturally I abjure this, as a Catholic, and indeed I never believed in it even as an ordinary Liberal. But we can use the word Nationalism, as

The Heresy of Race

I have used it all my life in defending Irish Nationalism. But *that* means exactly the opposite. It means
that nations should respect *each other's* nationality.
It means " The more I as an Englishman love England,
the more I should realise that an Irishman loves
Ireland ".

Now Distributists should note this point ; because
this Christian sort of Nationalism has the same plan
or ideal as Distributism. " The more your farm
is safe, the more my farm is safe ; a peasant exists
in a peasantry." Now it is a cold, hard historical
fact, quite apart from likes or dislikes, that the French
argued on Alsace, for instance, on this old morality
akin to private property, " Cursed is he that removeth
his neighbour's landmark ". And it is a cold, hard
historical fact that the Germans argued on an entirely
new theory of Race ; that a modern science of ethno-
logy revealed a superior Teutonic type, spread everywhere from prehistoric times, and wherever that type
could be recognised there the new German Kaiser
would stamp his foot crying, " This is German
Land ". Now it is simply not true to say that it was
the same on both sides, in this respect. France was
not in fact saying, " North Italy is full of round-
headed men looking more like Frenchmen than
Neapolitans or Sicilians ; all these Gauls must melt

into our Greater Gaul." No Frenchmen did say,
" Sooner or later the grand old Goths we call Spaniards
must be swept into our Frankish Empire." Once or
twice at long intervals, France has swept the world
with armies ; but always, rightly or wrongly, on the
old Catholic notion of spreading the alleged truth ;
never for an anthropological superiority of Race.
In the Crusades they spread Christianity ; in the
Napoleonic Wars they spread Equality ; but both these
ideas, when accepted, are applicable to all races. This
sort of Crusade may be a mistake ; but it is a rare
mistake and it is a Christian mistake ; Race is not.

In any case, as we can easily see, the far-off
French Crusades could not possibly apply to the actual
modern argument of France. That argument was
Nationalist only in the sense of Distributist. France
debated about France as French farmers debate about
farms. It is not a question of sentiment or preference ;
it may be possible to dislike a peasant haggling over
his fenced field more than a Bedouin chief wandering
over the world for conquest. It is none the less a
cold fact that the French argument was upon Catholic
principles ; that the claim was just ; that the landmark
was fixed ; that the property was lawful. It is quite
unquestionably a fact that the argument of the other
was on heathen principles ; that he was a favourite

of the gods, that pride in him was a virtue, and that his blood was more sacred than the blood of the brotherhood of men.

I think this wild worship of Race far worse than even the excessive concentration on the Nation, which many Catholics rightly condemn. Nationalism may in rational proportion help stability, and the recognition of traditional frontiers. But Anthropology gone mad, which is the right name for Race, means everlastingly looking for your own countrymen in other people's countries. And this character, which has every stamp of heresy, licence, undefined creed, unlimited claim, mutability and all that marks Modernism—this was wholly, entirely and exclusively on the Prussian side in the War. To put it shortly, Prussia stood for the Prehistoric; France stood for the Historic. Does any Catholic doubt which was the nearer to Catholicism?

XV

HITLER VERSUS HISTORY

AT the time of writing,[1] most people are rushing to the bookstalls to read about Hitler's violation of Locarno in evening editions and stop-press news. They would be much wiser to rush to the library and read volumes half a century old, about what their fathers and grandfathers thought of things now mostly forgotten. A famous scholar and humorist said somewhere, "When a new book comes out, read an old one." It is even more practically true to say, "When the latest news arrives, then go back to the oldest you can get hold of."

For there is now a cultural controversy far more fundamental than that between those who are Pro-French or those who are Pro-German; and it is the quarrel between those who are historical and those who are unhistorical. Those who would teach men how to hustle have only taught them how to forget. The effort to get the latest information means not so much information as ignorance; ignorance even

[1] On March 7, 1936, German troops entered the demilitarized zone of the Rhineland and Hitler denounced the Treaty of Locarno which Germany had signed in 1925.

of the origin of the information. So that there must be thousands of people to-day who really imagine that Hitler invented the racial arrogance now prevalent in Germany; or that his warlike demonstration without warning is something new in the international action of the tribe he leads; or that the situation is " unprecedented ", which is exactly what the sensational newsvendors love to call it, and exactly what it is not. The process is now nearly two hundred years old; and it began when Frederick the Great, by whose tomb Hitler like Hannibal dedicated himself to his heathen gods, shocked his own age by attacking Austria without a declaration of war.

The most piteous case is that of the Prussian Prime Minister, Goering, who seems to have said, " They say we do not observe our treaties; look at our treaty with Poland." This treaty has actually been running for more than a year; and the suggestion is that Goering has searched the whole history of Prussia for any other example of a treaty that was not broken. But I rather doubt whether the Poles even now draw deep breaths of confidence from the past memories of the attitude of Prussia towards them. But anyhow, the essential point to realise is that, whoever else is right, the person who is perilously and pestilently wrong is the person who says, " Oh

don't ask me to go back on all that old business about
Frederick the Great or Bismarck; really, it's almost
as remote as the invasion of Belgium!" He is building a somewhat insecure efficiency upon the mere
fact that he forgets what other people remember.

Any police-detective could teach a politician the
idiocy of this way of looking at a new mystery or a
recent catastrophe. When Mr. Brown has apparently
murdered Mr. Robinson last night, that is the exact
moment when the whole of their past lives become
intensely important; when it is most essential to
know whether the very first stages of Robinson as a
financier in South Africa offer any clue to his being
murdered; whether anything in the religious up-
bringing of Brown in Clapham encouraged or dis-
couraged him in the matter of being a murderer.
Only in high politics, only in those intense issues
of peace and war, only when millions of men may
be killed instead of one, do we encourage this incredible folly for forgetting the past. Only then do we
treat Robinson who has just been killed as if he had
just been born. Only then do we leave the question
of whether Brown is murderous entirely out of the
question of whether he is capable of murder.

Now when France, a nation admittedly desiring
peace, says in substance, "I cannot make a treaty

with a man who breaks a treaty as a preliminary to proposing it ", that nation is not standing on a point of law, or even indulging in a deplorable capacity for logic. That nation is remembering real events; real events that have recurred again and again; and it is merely common sense to say that its opponent is much too suspect already, to be allowed to treat an agreement as a form, as if the whole matter were merely formal. His conduct, in previous cases, has been (to say the least of it) highly informal. There is nothing in his own theory or practice to prevent him from invading France and proposing, from Rheims or Paris, a yet more universal and benevolent scheme of European reconciliation. We are dealing with facts; and the facts are in the foundations of history.

We have thrown away months of time, and masses of prestige, in perpetually advancing and retreating in some newspaper quarrel with Italy; simply because we would not say frankly that Italy was wrong in exactly the way in which we ourselves had been wrong. And all the time Prussianism had increased in prestige and power; and it is in an utterly different sense that Prussianism is wrong. Italy, like Imperialism in our own and other cases, has long sought to expand over less civilized countries; and while I am free to blame this in British Imperialists, I cannot understand how British Imperialists can blame it in Italian Imperialists. But all three can quite consistently blame the very special sort of thing that has long threatened Europe from the Prussian heresy poisoning so much of Germany. That is not an ethical controversy about whether civilized things may more or less control savage things. That is a pressing practical problem, of whether a more savage thing shall control more civilized things. In itself, the idea of our attacking a semi-civilized people is hateful to me. But the point becomes somewhat academic, when it is the semi-civilized people who may be successful in the attack.

To call Prussia or Prussianism a cancer has been considered rude, and even a term of abuse. In fact it is a cold and scientific statement. A cancer is a growth, which might grow like anything else, if it were anywhere else. What makes it a cancer is that it is an organism growing inside a superior organism; close to sensitive nerves or vital organs. That is the exact truth about this tribal pride, which might be not unnatural in Africa. It is not like the outward growth of the greater organism, civilization absorbing savages; wicked as that well may be. It is so placed that the things it devours are always more

108

valuable than itself; French or Flemish freedom or the culture and courtesy of Austria. That is what may be on the move and it is well to face it.

There may be any news when these lines are printed. Fortunately, what I say does not depend on any news. It has been true for generations and will probably be true for generations more: until some saint (more efficient than any army) converts a pagan tribe.

XVI

THE TRUTH ABOUT TRIBES

I HAVE just said that the charge of being a cancer, though not easily regarded as a compliment, has an objective and scientific sense which need not be connected with mere malice ; the sense of something that grows like an organism in the environment of a more valuable organism ; just as I found it necessary to point out on another occasion that the charge of being a fossil has also a more detached and delicate meaning that distinguishes it from mere vulgar abuse ; corresponding to a condition now very common in sects and political parties ; of being a mere shell or shape emptied of its first substance and since filled with a substance entirely different. I do not expect, however, that it will ever be possible to walk about calling my neighbours cancers and fossils and provoking only radiant smiles of agreement ; or to do so without considerable danger of misunderstanding. And the same difficulty applies to certain terms I have used about the tribal tendency, which may well appear more merely emotional or hostile than they really are.

I would point out that I never said that Germany

The Truth about Tribes

was a barbarian tribe. I said that there was a barbarian tribe in Germany. The fate of that great and mixed and often very valuable people has almost always turned on how far this tribal element has been permitted to become its spearhead or to use it like a spear. I do not know whether my words were those best adapted to express my meaning; but I do know that I have a very distinct and even dispassionate meaning; and that I know what I mean. It will be well, before any such misunderstanding perplexes us further, if I make another attempt to say what I mean. The point of the tribal spirit which haunts and inhabits, but only occasionally drives the Germans, resolves itself primarily into one fact; that it is a religion of Race. And there are two peculiar perils inherent in the cult of Race, which can be pointed out without any particular heat or hatred; as parts of the logic of history. The first is that this cult, for quite special spiritual reasons, tends more than any other to the nourishment of Pride. And the second is something which can almost be more spiritually perilous than pride: something that such visionaries call The Infinite; and those who have to deal with it call The Indefinite.

For the first, which is the more obvious; the curse of race religion is that it makes each separate man the sacred image which he worships. His own bones are the sacred relics; his own blood is the blood of St. Januarius. This makes patriotism something totally different from the enthusiasm for a flag or a charter or a shrine or an ideal commonwealth. That is a patriotism quite compatible with a passionate personal humility. The French or the Irish, for instance, have dark or ferocious vices tempting them all the time; but they do not in fact generally show this sort of worship of the racial image in the individual. With them the patriot loves his country as a man loves a woman; but not as a man loves himself. The ideal of France might be expressed in medieval times in a holy king or in modern times in the pattern of a perfect republic. But St. Joan of Arc thought more of the oil of Rheims even than of the blood of royalty; and she did not claim that she herself had royal blood. Every believer in the mere religion of race does inevitably claim that he himself has royal blood. A little French bourgeois in a café might believe in an Ideal Republic; but he need not think that he himself is an Ideal Republican. For sanctity and republicanism are not hereditary. Wherever we have the German Race religion, there is and must be the idea that heroism is hereditary. I do not mean for a moment, of course, that this heresy of heredity has only been known among Germans; it has been in various degrees the weakness of all hereditary aristocracies; and has only too much infected the aristocratic civilization of England. But it is true to say that the Germans have a sort of seriousness which is not English; and a sort of crudity which is not aristocratic. The consequence is that, given this belief, there is a tendency for every German, not merely to take Germany seriously, but to take himself seriously; because Germany is not an abstraction but a breed. It is not even an abstraction of blood and iron; it is an incarnation in blood and bone. It is a creed in which every man is his own incarnate god. In this very vital and practical sense the heathen Saxon is himself Wotan, is himself Thor. But a large ploughman from Kerry, or a large policeman from New York, does not think that he himself is a little dark rose; nor does a heavy old Norman peasant in wooden clogs suppose that his face and figure resemble St. Michael poised on his mountain above the sea.

The second way in which this racial heresy works havoc is this; that it is, as I have said, infinite and indefinite; precisely because it is not in its nature a plan like an abstract mathematical diagram; but a many-coloured map in which the colours all run into each other. The essence of Nazi Nationalism is to preserve the purity of a race in a continent where all races are impure. You can make frontiers and keep them like articles of faith ; but if you merely follow race wanderings, you will follow one tribe through a complexity of tribes, which you will always be trying to simplify by tales of extermination, colonisation or conquest. You will find German populations in the heart of Lorraine and may any time find them in the heart of Lincolnshire. For the various prehistoric, historic and unhistoric theories of migration or massacre will always enable you to treat all such subjects with too much simplification, precisely because they are really in far too much confusion. In short, if the patriot is more or less trained as a watchdog, he may remain inside the fence, even if he does not remain on the chain. But if the patriots are trained as a pack of hounds, to follow a scent blown upon any breeze, to go through all fences and across all fields, they are trained in a certain spirit which is quite certainly of some peril to their neighbours. In some moods and aspects, some may think the hound of the chase as noble an animal as the watchdog. But she is a somewhat different kind of animal ; and his habits are quite certainly different. That is what I mean when I talk about a tribal or even barbaric spirit present among Germans, and not necessarily present in all nations or all nationalists. And whether others agree with me or not, I am not merely slinging mud when I object to the ordeal by blood ; the blood-test.

XVII

THE RETURN OF PRUSSIANISM[1]

THERE are some who wonder how I came to pick up the strange fancy that Hitler and his colleagues are as warlike as they say they are, as narrowly nationalist and imperialist as they say they are, and as proud of the great period of the Prussian victories as every sane man knows them to be. I have seen a vast number of statements coming from their side; and the nearest to any note of peace, or even international justice, was an account of Hitler repudiating German War-Guilt over the tomb of Frederick the Great. Humour can hardly be his strong point; anyhow some of us are but little reassured by a man abjuring piracy over the bones of Captain Kidd or perjury upon the holy relics of Titus Oates.

But apart from Hitler's hero, who waded in war-guilt all his life, and scarcely pretended anything else, it would be easy for me to make a whole *dossier*

---

[1] In April 1933, G.K.C. wrote a letter to *The Times* under this heading. The Editor asked if it could be shortened. The author submitted a shorter letter, omitting much of what was in the first draft but adding some new sentences. The article as printed here contains elements of both the first and the second form of the letter.

of what Prussians and Pro-Prussian Germans are saying now. It is only a matter of looking up a lot of files; but I will mention two indications merely from memory. Hindenburg himself is reported as saying, "What has been German land must be German once more." Which means, and can only conceivably mean, that all the land that Prussia ever stole, in her most piratical and imperialistic period, Prussia now intends to steal again. In the case of Poland, for instance, the Prussian policy, at its most liberal, is simply this: that Prussia will generously give back to the Poles all that Austria and Russia stole from them, on condition that she can keep all that she stole herself. Does anyone in his five wits fancy this policy can be pursued without a World War? Or, to take a small popular indication, the streets were hung with banners inscribed "No honour without battle"; a very neat abbreviation of the well-known epigram of the German philosopher; "You say that a good cause justifies any war; but I tell you that a good war justifies any cause."

Nor need we look only among Prussians or Prussianists for these evidences of Prussianism. Count Montgelas, a Bavarian, a Catholic, a man writing like a cultured and humane gentleman, a man professing even to repudiate the old Prussianism

of Prussia, yet himself offers something like its most
extreme programme, as if it were a moderate programme ? I do not quite follow the reasoning by
which he desires the reunion of Austria with the
Reich, when he should surely desire rather the
reunion of the Reich with Austria. But anyhow, he
then calmly goes on to treat it as an equal tragedy
that " the Germans in Lorraine "—the province of
Joan of Arc—should be cut off from the Reich.
Bismarck himself doubted the annexations of 1870.
In this sort of thing, Count Montgelas seems to be
more Prussianist than Bismarck. The French word
Lorraine is traditional in all Western Europe ; indeed
he instinctively uses it himself. Outside the strict
Prussian State Schools, not one man in a thousand
even knows the German name for Lorraine. But
there are supposed to be " Germans " there ; and
wherever there are Germans he will wander with a
drawn sword to recover them. We shall soon hear
of his besieging Bradford.

I am not defending the bunch of politicians who
made the last Treaty ; and I assure Count Montgelas
that I have always denounced it for its stupid and
shameful destruction of Austria. I am defending a
historic fact ; for which thousands of the most
thoughtful Englishmen and Frenchmen, as well as

the bravest, died; the fact that Prussia has distorted the whole destiny of Germany and Europe.

We may all be wrong; God can bring good out of evil; and the new Bismarckian may complete his resemblance to Bismarck; he may go to Canossa. But if or when the New Germany moves one inch towards infringing on the present ancient frontiers of the Polish realm—then I shall know that I was right.

PART III
POLAND

XVIII

THE MODERN HYPOCRISY

IN all ages the world has rightly satirised religious hypocrisy. But in our age the world suffers terribly from something that can only be called secular hypocrisy. The cant is not only secular, it is even secularist. It acts on a fixed theory that religious motives, in national and international things, need not be calculated and must not even be mentioned. It is bad taste to suggest that the Sheik of Islam may possibly be acting in the interests of Islam; that the Zionist may occasionally think of the origin of the name of Zion; that a Quaker may sometimes be expected to act like a Quaker; or that it makes some difference, after all, whether a particular member of Parliament for a London constituency is a Parsee or a Plymouth Brother. All these shocking topics are covered over with a curious layer of godless respectability. It is not a question of liking or disliking any of the religions, or of having any religion at all. It is simply a taboo of tact or convention, whereby we are free to say that a man does this or that because of his nationality, or his profession, or his place of residence, or his hobby, but not because of his creed about the very cosmos in which he lives. This humbug is a horrible nuisance in any number of respects; and at present it is a horrible nuisance in the understanding of the political position in Europe after Locarno.

Poland is the Catholic culture thrust like a sort of long sword-blade between the Byzantine tradition of Muscovy and the materialism of Prussia. That is what Poland is; and that is infinitely the most real, practical, determining and important thing that she is. It is of more practical use as a political test than any other test we can propose. It is more of a description; it is more of a definition; it is more of a distinction. It is much more important than the fact that Poland is not Bolshevist; for the Prussian Junkers are not Bolshevist either. It is more important even than the fact that it has been a sort of favourite of France; though indeed the sympathy with France and the antipathy to Bolshevism are indirectly connected with this really determining description. For France has other allies linked to her by a similar policy; and in this case, as we shall see in a moment, these other alliances have much to do with the present perilous position. The point is that the element of religion is the element of realism. If anybody, who

The Modern Hypocrisy

knew Eastern Europe as filled mostly with Turks and Jews and Russians and North Germans and Lithuanians and so on, wanted to know what sort of people the Poles were, in a rough and ready but real fashion, he would learn a good deal of it, he would receive at any rate a guide and suggestion to help him in his estimate, simply by being told that they were Roman Catholics. If he had been in Italy or Ireland or Bavaria, he would know more or less what that meant; and he would to a definite extent be the wiser. He would not know everything about the Poles; but he would know something important about them. If he knew any history, he would get a new light on the talk about Polish chivalry, about Polish resistance to Communism, and all sorts of other things. But a curious sort of agnostic decorum forbids most of the modern press to discuss this dogmatic distinction in anything like plain English. It is not to be expected that everybody should like this eccentricity; but it is silly that nobody is even allowed to allow for it. There is a certain historical tradition in the West, which still has institutions and principles governing millions of people, and the Poles are among them. There are people of all sorts who dislike or distrust that tradition, often quite honestly, and that does in fact determine their practical attitude to Poles and Poland. We cannot for the life of us understand why there should be all this disguise about it. This is the sharpest of all the differences which divide a Pole from a Prussian or from a Bolshevist. This affects the nature of his quarrels with a Jew or a Russian reactionary. And this involves an imperfect sympathy between him and all sorts of worthy and well meaning people in Western Europe who happen to have a distaste for that type of spiritual and social life wherever they see it. They dislike it in Ireland and they would doubtless dislike it in Poland. What we cannot understand is why in the world they should not say what it is that they dislike.

Now none of these people will be able to make head or tail of what has happened to certain nations involved in the Locarno settlement, because they will never believe that their religion is relevant. If we were to tell them that there has been an ecclesiastical schism in Czecho-Slovakia, they would think it a small sectarian detail. If we were to tell them that the passion of France is always really a fight for theology, they would call it a paradox. If we were to say Caillaux is against Catholic France and therefore probably colder than many of his predecessors towards Catholic Poland, it would probably be

The Modern Hypocrisy

quite a new light in which to present that ingenious and unpleasant person. In other words, all these excellent and educated people have never really had a notion of what most of the continental conflicts are all about. They do not know what has given the colour to different countries; or why it matters when an ancient country like Bohemia is in that respect, for the time being, very much off colour. The French Freethinkers and the Bohemian schismatics have failed to support Poland, because they have only diplomatic and opportunist and privately patriotic reasons for preserving the connection with our outpost in Eastern Europe, and not the deepest motive of all. A French Nationalist Premier would have felt quite different; a Catholic Czecho-Slovakian would have felt quite different. They might have committed any crime, or even the same crime, but anyone understanding it would have known it was quite a different story.

Anyhow, there is no reason why people should not understand some of the real elements of the real story. The whole European problem has been profoundly affected by the recrudescence in France of the religious quarrel, round which that nation perpetually revolves. The return to power, by the rather artificial Parliamentary process, of some of the old

The End of the Armistice

Radical gang, whose anti-clerical hatred not only hardened but fossilised about a hundred years ago, has altered the international tone of France and of the allies of France. In most countries most people, who are very anti-clerical, tend to be rather anti-national; like the Orangemen in Ireland or the Huguenots in sixteenth-century France. Thus even when the French freethinkers are patriotic enough in their personal fashion, like Briand, they are part of a system that everywhere tends to be cosmopolitan. Anyhow the national France of Foch and Clemenceau and Poincaré was eclipsed by the semi-national, if not anti-national, France of Caillaux and Briand and the rest. And it is a simple historical fact that this anti-national France is also the anti-clerical France. About the same time as this change in France, and possibly as a part of it, occurred a schism in Czecho-Slovakia, whereby certain groups seceded from the Catholic unity. We are surprised that the English have not been told more of this affair, if only as a triumph of Huss and a New Reformation. It looks as if the British Protestants were wiser than some of the Bohemian Catholics. It looks as if England had realised by this time that a mere effort towards the Disunion of Christendom comes four hundred years behind the times.

The Modern Hypocrisy

Now in order to realise these things, it is not in the least necessary to take our view of them. It is not necessary to defend religion in order to realise the determining importance of religion. It is not necessary to defend religion in order to defend Poland. The case for Poland is quite practical; and can be put unanswerably to an atheist, if he is an opponent of Bolshevism and also of Prussianism. A man need no more be a Catholic to see such a solid fact than a British officer needs to be a Mahomedan in order to think the Turks are good soldiers; or to think it unwise to ignore Islam in India. It is for the sake of England and not of Poland that we appeal to all Englishmen to support Poland. But if anybody chooses to say that our religious sympathies make no difference, we answer that they do; and we make no disguise of it. If being of that confession is a thing that must be discounted, then it can be discounted. If that is what is called being partial, everybody can allow for our being partial. All rational English Protestants practically agree now that it was silly to crush Catholic Ireland; but anybody who likes can say, quite truly, that we sympathised not only with Ireland but also with Catholicism. So far as it is true, we have always put it truly; we put our cards on the table. What we complain of is that the cards of our opponent are so often up his sleeve, when he plays the good old game of Pope Joan. He always pretends that only political and social considerations affect him. He shrinks with a shudder from strong terms of attack and repudiation. We never denied that we hated Prussia, not of course in the sense of hating every Prussian, but in the sense of hating a positive political institution and wanting it weakened. But these people would never admit that they hated Poland. Oh no, my Christian brethren ! It is because they have a *true* sympathy for the *true* interests of the *true* Poland that they do not want her to have a port or a respectable frontier, that they hope piously that her army will be defeated by Bolshevists and her lands stolen by Prussians. And in the same way we remember very well having to contend with a number of people who had a true sympathy with the true interests of the true Ireland, for which the only hope was in the Orange Lodges. We never pretended to be fond of the Orange Lodges. But they could always pretend to be fond of the Irish peasants, while they were shooting and hanging and evicting them by the thousand. Love comes very easy to these people. It flows from them in all their books and speeches; indeed in everything except their actions. Those who are compelled to a Catholic

The Modern Hypocrisy

candour in their hatred are under a great disadvantage in these matters, as compared with this vast and placid plausibility; this hypocrisy of liberality, so much worse than any hypocrisy of bigotry. Under that disadvantage we shall remain.

XIX

THE HOPE OF THE NEW NATIONS

I HAVE come to have a sort of mystical feeling about the abstract justice of our case in the Great War. I mean that I am not less, but rather more, convinced that it was just. But I also mean that the feeling has grown more mystical and the justice more abstract; being abstracted from almost all the actors in it, even the actors on the right side. The medieval chronicler commemorating a Crusade (as it happens, a Crusade conducted by rather unscrupulous Crusaders) gave his whole book the magnificent title of Gesta Dei Per Francos; that is, Acts of God done through the French. I should call the Great War an Act of God done through the French, through the English, through the Russians, Serbs, Roumanians, Italians and Americans. But I doubt whether any of them quite understood the Act of God; I even doubt whether any of them were even worthy to understand it. I have never discovered the rag of a reason for reversing my original view of the facts. Unlike so many of my stolid, steady-going and conservative countrymen, I agree with every word I said a few years ago ; and I do not think that what was brutal barbarism as an experience has become beautiful brotherhood as a memory. But the point is not that the cause of the Allies was much better than the Germans'. The point is that the cause of the Allies was much better than the Allies. I do not doubt for a moment that we were right ; I know of no cause in history that was so right. But I have sometimes come to doubt whether we had any right to be so right. And what is true of England is true in various ways of her principal allies. We went into the War with the organ of government diseased with political corruption ; but the disease of the English Parliament was also the disease of the French Republic. And as France and England were governed by sham democracies, Russia was governed by only too real a despotism. It is open to anyone to dispute whether it is worse to be governed by Samuel or by Caillaux or by Rasputin. It is much more certain that Prussia was against liberty than that England was for liberty. It is much more certain that Prussia was against equality than that France and America were for equality. It is much more certain that Prussia was against religion than that Russia was for religion.

This growing notion of mine, that the Allies were not worthy of their work, is the very reverse of the

The End of the Armistice

pacifist reaction : the view that their work was not worthy of them. But it has received a sort of mystical confirmation from one strange outstanding fact. And that is the fact that none of those three, at least, have as yet got very much out of it. To a great extent, the good it has done has not been done to them. I am not, of course, forgetting for a moment the superb heroism of the French nation, any more than I am likely to forget the superb heroism of the English nation. But I am talking of something much more subtle and subconscious, like a sort of secret of history, whereby that noble effort was made to serve noble ends, but not necessarily their own ends. It is as if some divine irony had taken all diplomatists and demagogues at their word, and said : " You declare that your aims are not selfish. Very well, your rewards shall not be selfish. You shall only save something better than yourselves."

But when people go further and say that nothing was saved, that nothing was made better, all reason and reality contradicts them to-day. Mr. H. G. Wells says, or rather Mr. William Clissold says (we must speak by the card, or equivocation will undo us) that the Great War settled nothing and was as useless as a prairie fire ; a remarkable conclusion even to occur to one who guaranteed it to us as The War That

The Hope of the New Nations

Will End War. But Wells or William Clissold, or whoever made that second and opposite but equally sweeping statement, is quite wrong. The Great War has settled a great many things; has settled them on very firm foundations. The world is full of a number of quite new nations and institutions which were not there before the War, and would never have been there except for the War. The curious fact is that the nations thus benefited are not, generally speaking, the nations that waged the War. It may be argued that the Allies got little out of it; that Russia got revolution and England unemployment and France a financial problem. This is not an adequate description; but the thing can be so described. But it is nonsense to say that nothing was done for the new nations, when they were given their new nationality. It is nonsense to say that the Irish Free State is not a State at least freer and more Irish than anything from the time of Castlereagh to the time of Carson. It is nonsense to say that Poland got nothing out of it; when she got Poland out of it.

It is this particular case of Poland on which I propose to write one or two essays; and I wish to put first this general suggestion about her situation after the great catastrophe. It is open to anyone to grumble that the Irish and the Poles, whose attitude in the War was inevitably distracted and doubtful, ought not to have reaped where others had sown. I only remark here that my own instinct is for something greater and more mysterious than such calculation of merit; some memory of that voice that said : " Is thine eye evil because I am good ? I will give unto this last even as unto thee " . . . In some cases, perhaps even more.

XX

WHERE POLAND STANDS

THERE is one very real advantage, whatever the other rights of the case, in the recent break with the Russian Government;[1] or rather (to speak much more correctly) with the Government of Russia. And that is that it is at least addressed to real Bolshevists and not to imaginary Bolshevists. I am not very fond of that scheme of colour that mingles what is called the Red Peril with what ought to be called the Blue Funk. With the addition of the White Feather it makes a familiar tricolor; but I am not much inspired by that depressing manner of cheering for the red, white and blue. The common, not to say vulgar, manner of trying to beat a patriotic drum, so as to drown the cries of reformers alleged to be rebels, has always seemed to me in itself a silly business; and it seems so still. Everybody whom anybody happens to dislike, for any reason connected

[1] On May 27, 1927, diplomatic relations between England and the Soviet Government were broken off by a note which stated that the examination by the police of the premises of Arcos Ltd. and of the Russian Trade Delegation " has conclusively proved that both military espionage and subversive activities throughout the British Empire were directed and carried out from 49, Moorgate ".

with popular grievances, can be called a Bolshevist. Anybody who dislikes the wages of the poor being violently lowered by a lock-out is a Bolshevist. Anybody who dislikes the working classes being reduced to a servile status by a veto on strikes is a Bolshevist. Anybody who notices the mere obvious facts of nature, as that hunger is painful, is a Bolshevist. There is a great deal that is both curious and contemptible about this wild use of words; but one peculiarity in it stands out conspicuously from the rest. All the people who talk like that are talking as if there were no such things as real Bolshevists in the world. They are using the term as if. it had no reference to any actual state of things; as if a Red Russian were a fabulous monster merely to be used as a figure of speech; a thing to be employed only for purposes of fanciful comparison, like a dragon or a mermaid. It is very much as if people had been perpetually talking about Bohemians, merely in the sense of rather irresponsible artists; and had completely forgotten that there really is a place called Bohemia. So those who talked most about Bolshevism had really forgotten that there is a place that may be called Bolshevia. To break off connections with it is not perhaps a very vivid way of coming in contact with it. But it might perhaps serve to remind us of

Where Poland Stands

the people who, unfortunately for themselves, are permanently in contact with it. If people are really going to talk about the real Bolshevism of the real Bolshevists, the first thing they have got to remember is something that they have entirely forgotten. I see no evidence in any of the newspapers that have come my way that they have remembered it at all. I gravely doubt whether it has ever crossed their minds. It can be summed up in one word; and the name of it is Poland.

What stands between us and Bolshevism is an army; or rather a people in arms. There is one people, among all the peoples of Eastern Europe, upon whom Western Europe can really rely. The others have their virtues, like the Russians; they have their rights, like the Chinese; they have their particular claims and grievances, like a hundred other human groups in this bewildering world. But they are not, and perhaps never will be, a power to be permanently counted on for the protection of the old culture of Christendom, against this particular danger with which we are deafened day and night; the danger of Bolshevism. If Bolshevism really is such a danger, if it really is any sort of danger, then there is no doubt at all about what is the real protection against that danger. It is Poland; and the time may come when the protector must be protected.

The End of the Armistice

Suppose that during the Great War we had noticed that certain politicians were perpetually raving about spies while they were obviously indifferent to soldiers. Suppose they organised all London to chase a German waiter down the Strand or spent thousands in enquiring about an alleged Austrian hairdresser in Acton. And suppose at the same time they never sent a single pound of food or ammunition to the soldiers at the front. Suppose they forgot the very existence of the armies in the field. Suppose they almost denied the very existence of the armies in the field. Suppose they arrested a thousand clerks in Acton on suspicion of being hairdressers and imprisoned all the Fleet Street journalists because they were German waiters. And suppose that, all this time, they never mentioned the name of any British general or remembered the needs of any British soldier. We should not think very much of those politicians considered as patriots ; we should not profess a profound respect for their campaign against German propaganda. But this is pretty much what I think about most of our British campaign against Bolshevist propaganda. For the propagandists have forgotten altogether the Polish army which alone defeated the Bolshevists in the field.

I hope to say something in another article of less

obvious aspects of the position of Poland; but I
put this point first; because it is the most obvious
and the most completely overlooked. It is only necessary to ask any reader of the English newspapers,
familiar with this controversy about Continental
affairs, how often he has seen the word " Russia "
and how often he has seen the word " Poland ".
Western Europe is much more fond of talking about
its enemy than about its friend; I might say, so far
as Eastern Europe is concerned, its only friend. The
circumstances in Eastern Europe are so intrinsically
interesting that I make no apology for following up
these remarks with others; and anybody who is
bored with the real fight against Bolshevism in
Poland, and excited by the unreal fight against
Bolshevism at Westminster, is either a hypocrite or
he is strangely wanting in the historical sense.

XXI

THE CRIME IN WARSAW

I HAD just left Warsaw for about a week, and was
planning out a series of articles on somewhat more
serene and permanent aspects of Poland, when the
news reached me in Belgium of the political crime[1]
in the city I had just left. There is one aspect of
the affair that concerns the general position of Poland
very directly. The Bolshevists seem to be expressing
their very proper disapproval of a murderer by an
orgy of murder. But what interests me here is not
an orgy of murder, but an orgy of muddle-headed-
ness. Whether the Bolshevists are really so ignorant
of Western Europe, or whether they think it safe to
assume that those who hear them are ignorant of
Western Europe, they have certainly made the one
big mistake that can be made about it. By associating
England with Poland they make the deepest mis-
calculation that can be made. They imply an understanding between England and Poland which I most
heartily wish were really a fact; but which is unfortunately entirely a fancy. If we were as honest in

[1] On June 7, 1927, Voikoff, the Soviet Minister in Warsaw, was shot
dead by Boris Kowerda, a Russian youth of nineteen.

our Anti-Bolshevism as the Poles, then Poland
would be almost as important to us as it is to the
Poles. But as a matter of fact, I appeal to everybody
who reads our newspapers to say whether they make
Poland important. Poland was hardly ever mentioned in our papers until this Bolshevist tale could
be told against her. Warsaw was hardly even named
until an isolated individual crime happened to occur
there. Most of our people actually do not know of
the existence of Poland. An educated Englishman
wrote to a Pole the other day and addressed his
letter " So-and-so, Warsaw, Russia." I feel a deep
and glowing thankfulness in being able to say that
the Pole replied by addressing his letter " So-and-so,
Esq., London, Germany."

So when the Bolshevists talk of England's immediate intention of waging war on Russia, I am pretty
sure that they are either living in an unreal world
or appealing to one. I am not particularly horrified
at the idea of England going to war with the Bolshevists, any more than I am particularly in favour of it ;
England has gone to war for causes infinitely worse
and more wicked. But, as a matter of fact, I doubt
if it can be done. The mood of reaction against the
Great War is still much too strong ; or rather perhaps
too weak. I doubt if our younger generation who

The End of the Armistice

remember the Great War will go into a Greater War to express a newspaper disapproval of Socialism. There is very little Bolshevism in England. But there is a pretty large amount of Pacifism in England. I say it with grief; for I much prefer Bolshevism to Pacifism.

What England has got to understand is that the Polish case against Bolshevism is a real case. What Russia has got to understand is that the ordinary English case against Bolshevism is an unreal case. It is all the difference between talking about an abuse and merely talking about a term of abuse. It is the difference between talking of a Tammany Tiger and talking of a Bengal Tiger. To suppose that the speech of some cheap professional politician on the stump about the Red Peril, is in the same world with the wild crime of the poor fanatic in Warsaw, is to make the first and most fundamental mistake about modern Europe. Of that crime itself I shall have something to say elsewhere; but in this place it is enough to note that the same error is made by the Bolshevists and by the British Journalists; the notion that the Capitalist cant in our own country is part of the same movement as the military and religious defence of the remote borderland of Christendom. It therefore only serves to confirm the purpose I have in continuing to write on Poland.

XXII

WHY POLAND IS HATED

HAD I been able to write of all that lies between the towers of Cracow and the harbour of Dantzig, I might with luck have been able to give some hint of why Poland has been loved by so many heroes. But since I have no space to describe why she is loved, I must devote one more page to the more pressing and practical, yet the equally mystical and even equally glorious mystery; the question of why she is hated.

The trouble is twofold; first that most Englishmen know nothing about Poland and second that they never learn except from those who hate Poland—whom I strongly suspect of not being Englishmen at all. Anyhow their feeling is nothing less than hatred; of the sort only felt for very bad or very good things. There is a man on the *New Statesman* who every now and then breaks out about Poland. If we listened to a lecture at the London School of Economics, and the voice that went on for an hour or two, a little droning perhaps but very clear, were suddenly cloven by an inhuman howl like that of a

savage, we should have the same experience. It is
hatred. The same hatred is naturally a part of the
Bolshevist's hatred of Christianity and the Prussian's
hatred of chivalry.

The method employed, or rather indicated, in the
New Statesman was one often used in Imperialistic
and Conservative propaganda and familiar to all of
us who remember the old quarrel with Ireland. It
is summed up in the name of Ulster; and was known
among Radical satirists by the name of Ulsteria.
The method is this; when you can no longer deny
that a nation is a nation, and that it is or has been
an oppressed nation, you proceed to subdivide and
analyse its constituent elements, till you have found
a minority that can be represented as an oppressed
minority; or an oppressed minority that can be
represented as another oppressed nation. It can
always be found. By the very nature of all human
agglomerations, there is always a section marked off
by a difference; and sometimes by a very important
difference. The religious difference between Belfast
and Cork is a real difference; but the disadvantage
of the process continued indefinitely is—that it is
continued indefinitely. It ought in theory to make
an enclave of Catholics in Belfast as much as an
enclave of Calvinists in Ireland. I am not now talk-

ing of where it ought to stop in that particular case, or indeed in any particular case. I am only pointing out that anybody who hates a small nationality can pretend to be defending a smaller nationality; even if he really hates the first one because it is small or because it is national. The only check on the process is common sense or the comprehension of the normal; and those who hate nationality do not often understand normality. It is enough to say that there is always a difference between the actual and absolute national claim and the claims of these other groups, even when they are stated rightly and reasonably as the claims of groups.

The old trick that was tried against Ireland is now being tried by the *New Statesman* and other respectable papers against Poland. When I call it a trick I do not mean that no case can be made for it; I do not mean that it was wrong to make special arrangements for Belfast; or that it would not be right to make special arrangements for similar anomalies in Poland. As a matter of fact, many Polish statesmen, including the Polish soldier now ruling the State, are very sympathetic with the idea of such special arrangements. They would make very large concessions to the local discontents; so large as to make many of their nearer countrymen discontented. But I am talking about the true idea of a nation and the trick of playing the suggestion of a small nationality. And on this it is necessary for us, in the case of Poland as in the case of Ireland, to remain sane and to talk about realities.

Now standing where it does, Poland is not only a nation but the only nation. That is, it is the only nation in the western sense in which Ireland is a nation; or, for that matter, in which England is a nation. An exception may perhaps be made of Finland, which is westernised through other channels and something of its influence is now called Esthonia. But for the most part, the difference between the nationality of Poland and the nationality of White Ruthenia is exactly the difference between the nation of Ireland and the nation of Ulster. In that sense, the shortest statement is that one exists and the other doesn't. There is not the same type of traditional unity on both sides. There are people on both sides; and there are faults on both sides; and there are legitimate grievances on both sides. But the grievances are local grievances; they are not the story of a nation. There is one very rough but very practical test. Most of these excellent countries a few years ago were invisible on the vast map of Russia. Poland also was off the map; but she was very much on the spot. Three times she rose in revolution, until Europe rocked with insecurity; and everyone from California to the Caucasus knew the passion of the Polish exile. If there were any Ukrainian exiles, I do not think they managed thus to fill the world with the name of the Ukraine. If there were any Ruthenian revolutions, they were such shy and quiet revolutions that nobody heard of them outside Russia; if there was a Latvian war it must have been so very Latvian as to be called quiet and domestic. The truth is that nearly all these people were until quite recently simply Russians. But everybody in touch with reality knew the Poles were not simply Russians—especially the Russians.

This nation remained and rose again in a world of which nationality is not the normal character; and in which religion, race and language, while true and traditional and intensely interesting, are also horribly complicated and bewildering. It would be impossible for anybody to establish any workable state in those regions that would be free from these fringes of mixed population and international problem. The only difference is that the Poles are quite aware of the difficulties and rather anxious to solve them sympathetically; whereas the only two alternatives are the Germans and the Russians, neither of

whom ever dreamed even of pretending to sympa-
thise with subject peoples. In this connection a little
test will be found useful touching the journalistic
enemies of Poland. It will be found amusing to
enquire, touching those who weep for Lithuania and
Ruthenia, how many of them were heard weeping
for these states when they formed part of an enormous
empire. They are indignant on the assumption that
the edges of a country were nibbled by Poland. They
did not object to the whole country having been
swallowed by Russia—if there was any such country
to swallow.

PART IV
PACIFISM AND CYNICISM

XXIII

THE RELAPSE

AT a certain more or less definite turning-point, at a certain fairly measurable time after the Great War, something happened in nearly all the nations of the world. It had nothing to do with the Boom or the Slump ; it was not economic but ethical. I do not mean primarily to praise or to blame it, when I call it for convenience The Relapse.

It was a sinking of many societies back into their old ruts or their old routine, right or wrong. It was a paradox ; because it happened at the time, or immediately after the time, when everybody had been talking about Progress ; not only as if Progress were going on, but almost as if Progress would soon stop, having attained Perfection. It was the age of " noble experiments " ; the age of Prohibition ; the age when English politicians promised us a land fit for heroes to live in ; and when Pacifists anxiously added that never, never again, in this world, would there be a war fit for heroes to die in. A little boy was reported in the papers as having given up his toy pop-gun, and we all felt that Disarmament had really begun.

The End of the Armistice

Men became Gods in the last Utopia of Mr. H. G. Wells; and his Open Conspiracy was open to the most cosmopolitan conspirators. The American President spoke of making the world safe for democracy; not merely of making democracy, let alone American democracy, safe in the world. The League of Nations and the Fourteen Points, whatever their value, struck the same note of new and universal things. In short, up to that moment, men were thinking in terms of humanity and the whole world; and what had produced that larger outlook, whether you like it or not, was the War. In short, the nations had really become international in time of war. And then the nations once more became national—in time of peace.

I will not here discuss the reaction in America as an example of it; but it obviously was an example of it. The repudiation of the experiment of Wilson, the return to the maxim of Washington, the disentanglement from alliances, the dying down of definite partisanship for any of the European parties, are things of which many of my American friends strongly approve; but which I myself am in no particular position to judge. I only know that it was in this sense a Relapse; it was in any case a Return; and the casting away of certain almost

The Relapse

cosmic visions of co-ordinating other countries and cultures or (if you will) of minding other people's business. But in countries nearer home, of which I have much closer knowledge, what I call the Relapse is more remarkable still.

It was perhaps most remarkable of all in my own country. Everybody who knows any history, knows that the French and English understood each other far better when they fought each other at Crecy and Agincourt, than when they fought side by side at Mons or the Marne. Nevertheless, they did, on the whole, understand each other better at Mons and the Marne than they had, comparatively lately, at Alma and Balaclava. There was a real turn of the tide in English culture, appreciative of the long defence of Gaul against the Barbarians; it even found its way into a poem by Mr. Kipling and a speech by Mr. Lloyd George. For one brief and brilliant moment, it was really possible that the two oldest civilisations in Western Europe would be at least as friendly and enlightened as they were in the days of battle-axes and cross-bows. But that international vision, which shone for an instant in the very middle of the battle-field, vanished; and the two nations have now relapsed into being entirely national, or entirely narrow, as you choose to regard it. English caricatures once more contain idiotic pictures of impossible Frenchmen; and France, for all I know, may still refer to England as Albion. There is only one other application of this principle of the Relapse. It throws some light on the last news from Germany; and, for my own part, I fear it is a very bad Relapse indeed.

XXIV

ON CLEANING UP

I SHOULD like to say something of a matter which
the papers recently reported, in spite of its importance, and which the papers mostly approved, in spite
of its dire peril. I mean the business of the advance
and annexation effected by Japan.[1] That press which
prides itself especially upon being Imperial, hailed
the Japanese raid as supremely satisfactory, merely
because it was supremely successful. The publicists
who represent that opinion, after their usual fashion,
were quite sufficiently impressed by the fact that the
Japanese possess aeroplanes, armoured cars, tanks,
chemical gases or whatever may go to make a perfect
human culture. In comparison, it is undoubtedly
true that the ancient civilisation of China was in a
state of bewildering disorganisation and decidedly
inferior armament. It was, in fact, in that utterly
fallen, discredited and lost condition in which was
the so-called civilisation of Rome during that deplorable time of which the degradation is marked by the

[1] In January, 1932, Japan had launched the attack which destroyed
the authority of the Chinese Republic in Manchuria and ended by setting
up the puppet state of Manchukuo.

155

appearance of Augustine or Boëthius at the beginning, or of Charlemagne or Alfred at the end. Against
this chaos there did undoubtedly advance a body
drilled to the perfection of modern machinery and
specialising in all the tricks of the trade of modern
militarism. This more mechanical body managed
to establish itself definitely on land that belongs to
other people; and therefore, we are all perfectly
happy and the world is at peace.

Now, curiously enough, that is exactly how we
were all perfectly happy, that is exactly how the world
was for a long time at peace, under those successive
advances of the Prussian army which step by step
established the Prussian power—and the Prussian
problem. War went so smoothly that it seemed
almost like peace. Aggression and annexation pro-
ceeded so mechanically, on oiled and silent wheels,
that they really seemed quite natural and normal—
for those who did not suffer by them. Really, it was
hardly as if there was any war at all—except for the
people who were in it. The Prussians were so very
tidy in dealing with Silesia, with Poland, with Denmark, with Alsace, that our noble journalists actually
invented a beautiful term for such proceedings; they
still call it " cleaning things up ". On the other hand,
the older civilisation of Europe, like the older civilisa-

On Cleaning Up

tion of China, was very much more volcanic and incalculable. Poland was definitely discovered to be impossible ; because it was a place in which individual men insist on thinking for themselves. France was always liable to a Revolution. Whereas Prussia was obviously incapable even of a mutiny. That did not mean that it was incapable of a massacre.

But that was the practical condition of Prussianised Europe, which men treated for so long as the permanent promise of peace. Because Prussians always stand in rows to commit their crimes, it was obvious to every solid sensible man that they could not be really criminal. Because they always marked out the land they had just stolen from somebody else with a neat row of black and white posts (all of them, mark you, at exactly the same number of inches apart), it became obvious to reasonable men that there was no possibility of any further stealing. Because the success of Prussia against Austria, like the success of Japan against China, was the success of more elaborate armament and applied science, any sane man could see that the whole thing was over and there would never be any wars any more. In short, it was a matter of organisation ; and where there is organisation, my dear friends, there is order ; and where there is order there is peace ; and where there is peace there is justice; or if there isn't, it doesn't much matter. In a word, a certain sort of mechanical smoothness and swiftness is the test of everything; as it is the test of machinery. It does not matter that a man has a gun, so long as it is a machine-gun.

XXV

THE RIGHT TO ROB

A TRUMPET-BLAST to all the tribes of men, calling them once more to the grand old game of bodily combat and the resounding glory of arms, a stirring and inspiring clarion call to all humanity to throw all its chances once again into the great gamble of battle, a great call to the world to find again in War the supreme solution of all the paralysing problems of peace, a bugle blown to awaken all the ancient armies to rise from the dead and die once more in one huge heroic wrestle to seize the lands and cities of the world—it would seem strange if this came to us in one loud and eloquent cry, from that tower in which one of our most distinguished editors observes the world from China to Peru ; and at this moment, especially China. I myself was thrilled, but also startled ; for the argument appeared substantially to amount to this ; that Japan must go to war because she has a right to live ; that is, to live at somebody else's expense ; to live by stealing somebody else's country and carrying death into somebody else's home. Considered as a return to the old

The End of the Armistice

robust theory of The Struggle for Life, as Nietzsche and Henley preached it in my boyhood, I could even rejoice in it, with all the innocent humanity with which a boy can always listen to a bugle. What puzzled me very much was this; that this grand old doctrine that anybody may fight anybody, whenever he may think (or say) that his population is large or his commerce in difficulties, bore above it the mysterious or possibly ironical title, " Keep Out of War ".

It is interesting in many ways, but chiefly in this. It shows how everything that has followed on the War has broken down; but especially the case for Peace which was a reaction from the War. That case for Peace was put in various ways, but up to this moment it was always some milder or stronger form of the phrase; " Prevent War ". It is now saying exactly the opposite; under the caption of " Keep Out of War ". Men are even now discussing Disarmament seriously; up to about a week ago they were discussing the League of Nations equally seriously. Some have believed that everything could be settled by due notice and temperate deliberation; France and Russia have both proposed a Super-State, or at least a Super-State Department, with armies and navies that could prevent all other armies

The Right to Rob

and navies going into action. Mr. Wells would like
a World-State, which in its nature would presumably
wield from the centre whatever force was to be
wielded. One single blow of brigandage is struck
by a few Japanese Jingoes beyond the wilds of
Cathay; and all this is not only utterly abandoned,
but completely reversed.

For, whether it is realised or not, the argument
for the Japanese does mean abandoning all the world
to war. Once admit that old case for a cut-throat
Darwinism; that anybody may be a land-grabber
when he feels hungry for more land; and nearly
anybody in Europe, certainly everybody in Asia,
would imitate the Japanese to-morrow. This was
indeed the actual cause, or (what is more) the actual
excuse, of all the past aggressions and annexations.
The Prussians, that simple people, before the War,
believed themselves to be the aggressors; they prided
themselves upon having always been the aggressors;
they preached a serious Prussian philosophy of
aggression. The chief Imperialist journal of Germany, just as war was breaking out, said, " Does the
oak ask if it has a right to thrust its way through the
thicket ? " That is, the aggressor appealed to his
Right To Live, just as Japan is supposed to appeal
to its Right To Live; which may be more soberly

The End of the Armistice

described as its Right To Kill. All the argument for aggression and annexation, before the War, was founded on this theory that the teeming Teutonic populations must find an outlet; and must pillage Europe as the Japs will pillage Asia. I am not debating the ethics of this ethnic theory; to a Christian it can never be anything but a theory of theft and murder; but it is quite possible that to a Japanese it appears a legitimate tribal triumph. I need not deal here, as I have often dealt elsewhere, with the purely rationalist objections to aggression when it is called evolution, or the survival of the fiercest, when it is called the survival of the fittest. I only say that to justify Japan in such action is to justify the whole world waking up to activity in the same sort of action. It is telling every tribe under the sun that it is *not* to wait for arbitration; *not* to fear intervention; *not* to halt for one instant for any notion of international justice; but to kill quickly, in defence of the right to live. I know all about that philosophy; I think I understand it. What I do not understand is how, when we preach that philosophy to all the nations of the earth, any nation can expect in the long run to " Keep Out of War ".

XXVI

ON THROWING STONES

A SHORT time ago the spokesman of a militant
nation, speaking as a Japanese but claiming
specially to be a Christian, invoked the ancient
Christian text which is a defiance to the uncharitable ;
and said, " Let him that is without sin among you
cast the first stone ". I do not know whether he
understood all the questions he was raising ; but
he certainly was raising questions remote from war
or even politics, but very relevant to modern life.
His remark was quite just, of course, as a rebuke to
the Pharisaic sort of international insolence. It is
true of States as of citizens that we all like sheep have
gone astray ; and also that we all like wolves have
gone astray, devouring other people's sheep. But
people seem strangely to overlook, in the naturalness
of the retort, the acceptance of the accusation. If I
find it my painful duty to say to an Oriental poten-
tate, " You are a murderer ", the logical position is
not perfectly rounded off by his replying, " You're
another ". He may indeed be able to point to many
quiet little murders I have committed in corners,

especially in tight corners. He may even be able to bring in a final verdict of Guilty against me. But he is not even making the pretence of a plea of Not Guilty about himself. The whole point of the original Gospel story is that it concerned someone admittedly guilty and taken in the act; and this parallel seems logically to involve a man taken in murder, like the woman taken in adultery. The Japanese statesman really proclaimed in a loud voice that Japan is committing a sin; but that we are all miserable sinners.

But there is a wider application to a weaker side of the whole world to-day. By a gradual change from the pre-war sentimentalism to the post-war cynicism, which has been the chief change of recent times, the notion of forgiving sins has turned into the notion of forgetting sin. The one thing that seems to be entirely missed, in such appeals to the sayings of Christ, is the final point of what Christ did say. Although the sinners dared not throw stones, and even the sinless did not condemn in the judicial sense, certain words were used which had a much more practical sense : " Go and sin no more ". To judge by many modern references, one would suppose that the whole scene ended with the words, " Go on and sin as much as you like ". Thus the parallel would be quite perfect, if we can suppose that authority (which the Japanese gentleman avowedly accepted) saying to him and his Government, "You are no worse than other Governments; there is no nation which has that sort of right to condemn you; neither do I condemn you. Go and shoot no more. March no more. Invade provinces and invest towns no more. In a word, never mind whether they are sinners or not; but do you sin no more". That would be a perfect pattern of fulfilment of the parallel which the Japanese gentleman himself invoked. But it would result in a very abrupt military movement and highly unexpected developments in the politics of the Far East.

XXVII

THIRD THOUGHTS ARE BEST

THE outlook in Europe is dark; and it looks as if the Pacifists will succeed in dragging us all into War. For ever since the end of the War That Ended War, the pressure for a renewal of hostilities has come almost entirely from those who profess the ideals of internationalism. It will be noted that the very word Internationalism has come to stand for certain nations against other nations. It is Internationalism to want an understanding between England, America and Germany. It is Internationalism to want an understanding between England, Germany and Russia. But it is not Internationalism to want an understanding between France, Poland, Hungary, Czechoslovakia, Serbia, Italy and England. That is Nationalism, and not Internationalism. I cannot imagine why. I am quite well aware that there are any number of good and sincere men, who really desire peace in Europe, and whose European sympathies are rather different from mine: but I cannot understand the particular type of journalist who has ever since the Great War made himself the most noisy spokesman of cosmopolitanism. A united Europe which leaves out France and Italy seems to me rather like a complete man who has forgotten to put on his head and body. And a broad-minded sympathy with all nations, which manages to be blind both to Rome and to Paris, seems to me a little difficult to distinguish from the blindness of barbarism. I know that there are good Christians and good Catholics, who desire the unity of Christendom as sincerely as I do, and who have been from the first quite honestly on the side of Germany and Austria; for that matter, a large number of them presumably live in Germany and Austria. I know that there are Englishmen who love England as strongly as I do, who have yet thought it the wiser English policy to be on the side of Germany since the conclusion of the War. There is always this problem of the respectable and the dubious upholders of a sympathy or a policy. But I do think that the time has now come for these groups, and especially the latter group, to consider very seriously where their sympathy and policy have actually led them. God alone can judge the heart; and it is not impossible that we are sometimes wrong, when we try to distinguish the peacemaker who inherits the Beatitude from the peacemonger who defiles the

Temple by selling doves. But we can, assuming the sincerity of the heart, call for some serious responsibility in the head. And we can ask men of all opinions to note very seriously indeed the actual steps and the actual story of international policy and diplomacy since the great conflict; and to consider what light they throw on the two theories of the reconstruction of Christendom.

There is a general view of the European elements, which I held before the Great War and have never substantially altered after it. I freely admit that, like all other generalisations about political problems, it is patched all over with exceptions and incongruities; but I think it was broadly true. It was the view that the Allies (most of them probably without knowing it) were fighting for the old core of European culture against things cruder and more destructive in the North. Whichever way you read such a medley, the exceptions always seem as large as the rule; and this rule was counterbalanced by all sorts of things; notably by Austria and Bavaria, which really were of the old culture, being dragged at the tail of Prussia, the captain of the new. Indeed, though Austria was utterly unscrupulous in her ultimatum to Serbia, yet if the War had *only* been Austria against the Slavs, my description and even my sympathies would have been different. But the West was the world in peril; and the two realities of the West were Pagan Prussia and Roman Gaul. That at least was and is my view; and I now ask everybody to consider what has actually followed on following the other view.

Prussia has proved her Paganism once again in the Nazi movement; as for that matter in the Nudist movement or half a hundred heathen fads. But above all, in this vital or very deadly fact; that the *Nazi is ready to dally with Communists*. That is the flash of fact and reality that blasts all sorts of labels and conventions. The Nazi may be Nationalist and the Bolshie may be Internationalist, but these are words; for Prussia is hardly a full nation and Russia is much less in contact with other nations than anything else. But they both feel they are of the same stuff; a stuff which they would call the new forces and I should call the old barbarism. The Prussian patriot may plaster himself all over with eagles and iron crosses, but he will be found in practice side by side with the Red Flag. The Prussian and the Russian will agree about everything; especially about Poland. They may differ in many things, but in hatred of the Christian civilisation they are truly international.

Second, the moment the War was over, certain forces which, on any argument, are somewhat alien to old Christendom and the Catholic instinct, instantly rushed to the help of Prussia. The usurers were all Pro-German; even those innocent usurers who are now rather too bewildered to know whether their complicated and incompetent financial system is usurious or not. New York, and especially all that was most cynical and least traditional about New York, was the seat of the financial force directed in this way. It was instinctively and almost universally felt to be the enemy of Europe. And it was this enemy of Europe that was the friend of Prussia. Well, we have seen what sort of a financial effect was produced by those financial experts. It was because these men, alien to Europe, had therefore a weak favouritism for Prussia, that they let us in for our biggest financial crash when Prussia flatly refused to pay. Seen clearly, without excuses of reconciliation or reaction, the Prussian has actually acted since the War exactly as we charged him with doing before the War and (barring some newspaper lies) during the War. He has not acted, certainly he is not acting, as a friend to Europe.

Lastly, there is something abroad in the streets, very loud, very living, violently excited, that is telling lies against Poland. Lies that it cannot defend; lies that it does not retract; lies that it dare not leave

Third Thoughts are Best

open to printed criticism. Whoever be the liar, and whatever be the origin of the lie, it is being circulated in order to break down the wall of Christendom, which is called Poland, and alone guards us against an Asiatic anarchy, as it did against the Tartar hordes. I very earnestly ask my fellow countrymen, and especially my fellow Catholics, to turn these three things over carefully in their minds.

XXVIII

ONE WORD MORE

IT is hard not to suspect some journalists of the generous dream of making a European war and keeping out of it. Thus we should grow as rich as America was; and then be ruined as America is. That is their bright idea of saving Capitalism. I therefore propose to add this postscript upon the international position, and to explain more fully what I mean by considering anew the truths behind the national position of 1914, and the curious way in which we may yet come back to them. That is what I mean by saying that third thoughts are sometimes the same as first thoughts, and much better than second.

But first it is necessary to insist that my view has nothing whatever to do with Jingo journalism or war-fever or flag-waving or any sort of internationa hatred. It has nothing to do with our vice of despising our enemies, or our much greater vice of not despising ourselves. Above all, it is not any sort of journalistic war-howl against " Germany " or " Germans ". Our cheaper journalists knew no history, and were only torn between denouncing Germans as cannibals and admiring them as chemists. In so far as " Germans ", if not " Germany ", represent a reality in European history, in that sense and in that degree Prussia was simply a revolt against Germany. The Hohenzollerns were a belated mutiny against the Hohenstauffens. The thing that troubles Europe is something that was really Anti-German as well as Anti-European. The trouble is not that there are many millions living in the middle of Europe, with more or less light hair. The trouble is that a particular patch of the Baltic Plain was always too far away from the German Empire, as well as the Roman Empire. Its nearness to the Balkan ports gives it a sort of cold cosmopolitan activity, like a very remote colony, while leaving it unwarmed by the more glowing cultures of the South, the vineyards, the shrines, the chivalries and charities of the Faith. This patch of what we call Prussia, like many patches of what we call Russia, is and has long been a bitter breeding-ground for crude and cranky ideas ; a dark and tangled garden of tares and thorns and thistles, on which long-eared professors still solemnly feed. To see the point, we must forget all the big imperial and national labels that modern journalistic history pastes across the map. We must rather imagine we

The End of the Armistice

are dealing with some strange strip of culture in Asia
Minor or Mesopotamia, which was a seed-plot of
heresies or inhuman cults in the cosmopolitan world
of Antiquity or the Dark Ages. We do not get even
near the nerve of the truth, by talking for or against
" Germany ". Many German elements are among the
best European elements. I warmly agree that the
Centrum has been the key-fort of civilisation and
peace, for long periods since the War ; but so it was
on any number of occasions before the War. The
point is that the Nazi is the enemy of the Centrum,
as it is the enemy of the civilisation the Centrum
protects. Nor is it the point to complain that the
Nazi is Nationalist, as an Irishman is Nationalist or
a Pole is Nationalist. The whole point about the
ideas born in this borderland is that they are *not* the
normal and traditional prejudices of the older nations.
They always have about them that fatal illusion of
freshness which belongs to half-baked culture, to
cheap new religions, to cocksure colonial policies, to
the black man who is proud of wearing a top hat
and the white man who is proud of not wearing
anything. These people are always led deeper and
deeper into the mire by their favourite word " Forward! " It was the title of a militarist paper before
the War, run by a Jingo Jew who told Germany to

174

break through Europe as an oak breaks through the thicket, without thought of right or wrong. Towards the end of the War, when Germany really needed defending, the Jew became a Pacifist. When I think of that particular sort of Jew, I can understand Hitler being an Anti-Semite. But he is none the less a fool to fall back on believing the Jew's first lie, which the Jew himself had to abandon.

Nobody who knows anything about Berlin will say I am entirely wrong, when I decline to discuss it as a German town like Cologne or Nuremberg. Anyone so informed will know what I mean, when I say it has long been a city of very strange gods, not to say demons ; as if it were an Asiatic city just outside Christendom. The danger of the Nazi crisis is that it may mean a renewal of the abnormal and anarchical notions, that thrive in the cold unrest which blows like an eternal east wind upon that Baltic shore. Whether it was the atheism and ape-like energy of Frederick, whose ambition was a hungry hollow not to be filled, or whether it was the white nightmare of the Superman, pure and spotless as Antichrist ; whether it was the Kaiser wearing a mailed fist or Professor Goggleheimer wearing nothing with equal earnestness—there was about this narrow Northern culture something not quite

The End of the Armistice

human. We knew it when we were fighting it; and though our journalists told the filthiest lies, they told some truth—which was equally filthy. Remember that though the word "Hun" became mere vulgar abuse, it was history. The Kaiser did actually tell his soldiers to behave like Huns.[1] It could not have been said by any other Christian prince of any other European people. It could not have been said by much worse kings in touch with European history. It would have been like telling us to do the work of the Black Death; or to model ourselves on the microbe of the cholera.

It is necessary to repeat such history, because history is repeating itself; because it will seem new and monstrous and unexpected that history should repeat itself. We have used fire and sword, death and destruction, slander and surrender, diplomacy and flattery, suspicion and oblivion, to solve the supposed problem of Germany; and we find that we still have not solved the problem of Prussia. The reason is that the thing involved belongs to the history of

[1] After the assassination of the German Ambassador to China during the Boxer rebellion of 1900, the Kaiser addressed his troops at Bremerhaven as they were about to sail to join a punitive force. He used these words: "As a thousand years ago the Huns under King Attila gained for themselves a name which still stands for a terror in tradition and story, so may the name of Germany be impressed by you for a thousand years on China so thoroughly that never again shall a Chinese dare so much as to look askance at a German."

thought, to the thousand sects and philosophies, rather than to the relatively recent imperial divisions of history. The thing is not a nation; it is rather a religion or perhaps an irreligion. Perhaps, after all, it is ultimately an ignorance. But it is the sort of ignorance that calls itself agnosticism; and is certain that it knows everything.

XXIX

THE END OF THE PACIFISTS

THE world has long debated whither the world
is tending; and the queer thing at this moment,
as it seems to me, is that it is at present tending to
nothing. Yet I mean by nothing what might be
called a positive negative; as distinct from a negative
negative. I mean that it is drifting in a direction;
but in the direction of a void or an abyss. The most
curious feature of the time is the continuous soft
collapse of one thing after another, like sand castles
sapped by the sea; of almost everything except (as
I should say) of one tradition of truth that is not
of this earth and certain hard facts that are very
specially of this earth; such as the fact that food
comes from the earth and from nowhere else. Outside these, the most remarkable spectacle is the quite
rapid senility of quite recent things. It is the swift,
silent decay and decrepitude even of the things which
only yesterday were recognised as new, even if they
were resisted as new; or repudiated and reviled as new.

For instance, it is stale stuff now to say that we
have abandoned the Pre-War standards and ideals.

The End of the Pacifists

The point is that we are now abandoning the Post-War standards and ideals. It has nothing to do with what I happen to like or dislike; some of the dreams of Reconstruction after the War seemed to me visions of real civic justice; some of them seemed to me nightmares of negative cosmopolitan centralisation. But most men are not now in the mood of those priggish constructive ideals, any more than of the more manly ones. In the year 1914 most normal men were organised and resolved to wage war. By about the year 1924 most normal men were organised and resolved to prevent war. But go among ordinary normal men to-day, and see how many of them have any heart to try, or any hope to succeed, in preventing a huge war breaking out in Asia and perhaps rolling towards India. I have in my time criticised Pacifism; but at this moment I wish there were anything so positive as Pacifism to criticise. What there is, is not Pacifism but simply pessimism; a paralysis of the world in the presence of a new war of the world. What has become of all that urgent unanimity that not only preached the League of Nations as the last word of the law of nations, but imposed it on our own nationals as a part of the British Constitution; enforcing it through the State schools and the ministerial platforms, and setting every tiny tot to

179

wave the white flag in one hand and the Union Jack in the other? What has become of all the prophecies of the modern prophets, and the clear demonstrations of the impossibility of war, repeated incessantly by some of the clearest and ablest writers of the age? Has the Open Conspiracy closed down or completely shut up shop? What has become of the World State, and has it no concern with the state of the world? In the case of many of the chief spokesmen of the reaction against the Great War, we may say that they fell at once into a complete reaction against the reaction. By the time the challenge from Japan came to all the internationalists, these men were ready to talk, not internationalism nor even imperialism, but simply barbarism; or at least a barbaric fatalism that fell back on the law of the jungle; or rather the lawlessness of the jungle. One of our editors, as we have seen, actually acquiesced in the Japanese assault on the world's peace, to the extent of saying that a nation had a right to live. That is, it had a right to live in contempt of right. But this extraordinary collapse from idealism into cynicism was negative rather than positive. The principle obviously opens a vista of unending invasions and aggressions, for ever and ever. But I willingly believe that it was in sheer weariness that

The End of the Pacifists

he threw open the gates of war, and abandoned the world once more to eternal anarchy.

It is true that in this particular case there is a very curious unconscious irony; not without a sort of hooting echo of devilry. It is horribly bad luck for a certain type of peacemonger that the powers declaring war are those with which he would most desire to be at peace. When men hold a certain sort of philosophy, which is really the materialist or mechanistic philosophy, they have a strong natural sympathy with the sort of order established by Prussia or Japan; as I should say, the sort of tyranny established by Prussia or Japan. They quite sincerely prefer peace; that is they would prefer that order, or that tyranny, to be universal and undisturbed. But they cannot help preferring it, even when it is disturbing the peace, and long before it has dictated the peace. It is a long story; it is largely connected with the fact that all *copying* has a kind of neatness and precision that is less obvious in creative things. The tracing of a drawing has a hard and clear line, compared with which the original sketch looks too sketchy—and too original. A copying-machine may not only copy exactly, in the common sense; it may produce something that looks more exact than what it copies. Now the two great copyists in human

history are the Prussians and the Japanese. Their
triumph is not merely the triumph, their cause is not
merely the cause, of militarism or industrialism or
imperialism; it is the cause of plagiarism. Prussia,
as distinct from Germany, was very pale and colour-
less when she was artificially painted with the colours
of French militarism, and then of English navalism,
and now, apparently, of Italian Fascism. Japan has
more credit and discredit; for she had a beautiful
background of her own old Oriental colouring;
when she chose to splash it all over with the vulgar
paint of publicity and commercialism. But they are
both geniuses in imitation; that is, in industry and
detail, and a certain dullness and lack of defiance.
People who have a mechanist and fatalist religion
are fond of that sort of thing. God knows how they
manage it.

Anyhow, the point is that it is not merely the
Pre-War ideas, it is pointedly and specially the Post-
War ideas, that have collapsed at the first whisper of
war. Supposing that nothing remains of the national
unanimity in face of the World War, what has become
of the international unanimity in favour of the World
Peace? Supposing we are agreed, for the sake of
argument that Victorian obligations of virtue and
patriotism, and living with your wife and dying for

The End of the Pacifists

your country, were all very antiquated and absurd, what is to take the place of the obligations that were once supposed to take their place? Granted that enlightened youth, reading nothing but dirty novels by deserters and panic-mongers, can have nothing but contempt for the courage of the Volunteer, what has become of the courage of the conscientious objector? What at least has become of the peace he hoped to impose on the world? It would be laughably unfashionable to hint that there still lingers something sacred over that great grave of a million men, who did the last thing that men can do for their own land and for liberty. But what has happened to all that other army, that only survived to swear that it should never happen again; that nobody should be allowed, far less encouraged, to let it happen again? Have they all been hard at work, persuading the Germans of the injustice of attacking Poland; pinning the Japanese with the infamy of attacking China? They are always talking about the old men who blundered into war; have the young men done anything to avoid blundering into war? Alas, in this case it is the rising generation that is a falling generation; and with less dignity, as some still strangely feel, than if they had fallen in war.

183

XXX

HIDING AN EARTHQUAKE

THE world is in a condition of earthquake and
eclipse, combined with an enormous irony of a
failure to realise that these portents have happened
at all; a condition which I try in vain to express by
any figure or form or logical contradiction. The
weirdest part of the business is the way in which the
old discussions go on under the new conditions;
merely because they began a long way back under
the old conditions. It is as if a new Ice Age had
clutched our whole planet, so that the very seas and
oceans were all solid skating-rinks; and we had to
listen to an endless public debate between the British
Blue Water School, demanding the command of the
sea for our own ships and the opposite school demanding the freedom of the sea for all ships. It is as if
the Deluge had returned; and the last mountain-peak
were submerged, and we were all floating about in
boats and rafts, shouting at each other about the
urgency and practicality of our alternative policies
for the division of land. Many will feel this to be
an exaggeration; partly because mere language masks

what has happened, but still more because even what has happened is not an adequate description of what is happening and most people find an uncanny sort of quiet in the mere fact that nobody knows what will happen next.

To take only one example; the men who argue about medieval history still go on arguing upon the same point; which is, broadly speaking, how far, or how soon, the ancient spirit of slavery was transformed into something more like the spirit of peasantry; in what sense even the serf may have felt himself the owner of his strip of land; how far the rabid application of Roman Law by the lawyers was felt to be false to the facts of the age; and so on. Men much more learned than I are engaged on both sides of this controversy, and I am not now concerned to decide it, even if I could. But, whatever was the positive quality of medieval serfdom, nobody notices that the relative quality of medieval serfdom has undergone a huge upheaval of change, within the last year or two. I mean that everyone judging medieval serfdom compared it with modern employment; and nobody notices that the whole case is altered, in proportion as we have nothing to compare it with, except modern unemployment. The feudal system was a method by which millions of

people were fed on the land. It had all sorts of other
evils and vices which I should heartily admit; but
even if it had all the evils and vices that I should
flatly deny, even if it had all the evils and vices that
its most violent and fanatical critics could impute
to it, it would still remain the fact; that it was a way
of feeding millions of people on the land. The serfs
may not have had the best of food off the land; the
serfs may or may not have had the inner indescribable
sentiment that goes with owning the land; but it is
a fact that all or most of them had some land; and it
is certainly a fact that all or most of them had some
food. Now the possibility that is opening before us,
in the modern world, is something that up to a few
years ago everyone would have called an impossibility. It is the possibility that modern Capitalism,
when it completes its cycle, may turn out to have
been simply a way of separating people from food,
as it has certainly been a way of separating people
from land. Its chief achievement will have been to
create an extraordinary unnatural alternation of glut
and famine, which means that in good times food is
brought from afar by a certain machinery; and in
bad times the machinery breaks down and the food
is not brought at all. It is a mere matter of brute
logic that this means, at the very least, that a tragedy

might happen in a modern city, which could not possibly happen in a medieval manor. The lord of the manor might hang some of the serfs because he was annoyed with them; but he could not possibly starve all the serfs, merely because he did not need them, for obviously he did need them, there being then no other way of getting food out of the earth. Now the mere existence of this as a possibility, a thing threatening us even with partial fulfilment of such a fate, alters the whole argument; not only about serfdom, but for that matter, even about slavery. It is no good arguing on fixed assumptions about how bad the medieval system was, and how good the modern system is. We simply do not know how bad the modern system is. We do not know how far the failure of the brief commercial prosperity will go, in the way of a dangerous division and distance between a man and his dinner. We only know that this is the first system that ever did divide him from his dinner in that distant and dangerous way. It is useless to compare such colossal collapse with anything normally meant by failure or famine. There is no past parallel to a world so closely knit up by communications, in which such a contradiction can exist as that of the infinite threat of over-production and machinery. We are destroying food because we do not need it. We are starving men because we do not need them. Men might well go back to a more than medieval slavery to avoid that lunacy. Men may yet go forward to a Bolshevist slavery to avoid it.

Another example, besides the debate on Medievalism, is the debate on Militarism ; and that fine fighting patriotism which is much more really military than Militarism. Since the war, the praise of both the best and the worst military spirit has been covered with a rather thin and wordy Pacifism in nearly all countries. If hardly anybody actually praised Prussianism, since that was to praise Militarism, yet neither was anybody allowed to blame Prussianism ; for this might give rise to an outburst of patriotism ; nay, perhaps, to some dangerous indulgence in courage and independence. So we were all taught to agree that France and Germany were very much alike, especially Germany ; and that everybody is a Pacifist, especially a Prussian. Above all, there has sunk over this country especially a bewildering silence and sick indifference, about the heroic memories of the men who did undoubtedly wage the war as a war of justice ; the heroes and the poets and the good citizens who died for a vivid conviction that Prussia was Prussianism and Prussianism a poison to the world. At the best, everybody has been vaguely arguing that, since then, so much water has flowed under the bridges that it is no longer necessary to hold the bridge-heads, so that we can comfortably forget the very names of Horatius or Herminius or the heroes who kept the bridge. And people still continue to talk in that way down to this very moment, and cannot see the staggering alteration in the European landscape, which stares them in the face; which, in fact, has just happened before their very eyes.

For the truth is that what has really happened has completely justified the theory of Europe on which the Allies went to war. At least this is true of the good Europeans among them, who were intelligent enough to have any theory of Europe. These people thought that Prussia (not Germany) was a permanent threat to the peace of the world; and they were perfectly right. They were right then, and they would be right now. Prussia was a threat to peace then; and she is a threat to peace now. If they were wrong, it was because they did not succeed in removing the threat; not because they were wrong in thinking it threatening. But that was because the mere perverse reaction of Pacifism and Pro-Germanism led us to support our late enemies upon every point and thwart our late Allies in every particular.

189

The End of the Armistice

The result is that Prussia begins to reappear; which means that Militarism begins to reappear; which means that War begins to reappear. Prussia means Prussianism now exactly as it meant Prussianism then; it always did, it always does, and (short of a spiritual conversion) it always will. Prussia is a patch of eighteenth century heathenry and heresy, which never did believe, nor (to do it justice) generally pretend to believe, in any sort of international ideal or common code of Christendom. From the first command of Hohenzollern to the last appeal of Hitler, it is the most simple, one-sided, savage tribal patriotism; and nothing else. The consequence is that Prussia is the one European State that may at any moment wage an aggressive war. We all said this steadily for five years; not all of us mixed it up with the lies of the Yellow Press; and some of us have always refused to unsay it. But a good many seem to have been ashamed for ten years of having told the truth; and are still ashamed, even when the truth has once again come true.

XXXI

ON WAR BOOKS

I FEAR that the poet Campbell is largely forgotten,
though many things about him may be and should
be remembered. He wrote *Hohenlinden*, a rattling
good battle lyric, with a rhythm really like the rushing of horses. He testified to a better age of English
liberal opinion, by writing the hackneyed lines about
the destruction of Poland, and how freedom shrieked
when Kosciusko fell. I do not know whether anyone remembered it when the nation regained its
rights; there was certainly no doubt that pedantry
and hypocrisy shrieked when Kosciusko rose from
the dead. I need not make a further parade of the
very few facts I know about Campbell. He used to
wake people up in the middle of the night with an
idea for a poem, and demand tea; a questionable
habit. But there is a story told about him which is
now something of a parable. In other respects, I
imagine he had the normal notions of his time and
country, and was not insincere in his patriotic poems.
It was therefore the more surprising to the company,
when he rose to his feet at a dinner of English literary

men, in the middle of the great war which included Hohenlinden and The Battle of the Baltic, and proposed the health of Napoleon Bonaparte. A storm of protests broke; but Campbell calmly waved them away. " I will admit," he said, " that the Emperor is a usurper; that he is the enemy of our country, and if you will of the whole human race. But, gentlemen, let us be just to our great enemy. Let us not forget that he shot a bookseller." Here again, of course, he spoke under the conventions of his time. Nowadays, meaning the same thing, he would have said a publisher.

Animated by the same principles, I solemnly lift my hand and say in tones of moving sincerity and emotion " Heil Hitler! " And, in case this causes any such momentary surprise as was stirred by the toast of Mr. Campbell, I hasten to explain the special cause of my feelings. Herr Hitler and his group have done many things of which I cannot approve. They murdered a number of people without trial during a sort of week-end trip. They murdered a man merely for being an influential Catholic; and, what is even worse, explained that they had murdered him by mistake. They beat and bully poor Jews in concentration camps. They talk about preserving the purity of their blood. They commit every crime.

On War Books

But let us be just to our great enemy; or to all our enemies, great or small. Let us not forget that they did destroy, not a mere bookseller, but a book. Let us not forget, in fairness to them, that they did make a bonfire which burned to ashes a very much boomed book called *All Quiet on the Western Front*.

This service to literature was the nearest that Germany will ever come to atoning for setting fire to the library of Louvain. For the booming of books of this sort, noisily and needlessly, is quite as much a mark of our times as the making of better books, decently and modestly, was of the times to which the library of Louvain looked back. We all know the marks, I might say the trade-marks, of this type of modern production. First of all, it is always in the manner of mass production. It is generally a big book, demanding big publicity, big circulation, big choruses of reviewers; in short, it is the sort of great literature that is best managed by big business. I remember many such books that were merely booms. Lombroso's brutal rubbish about criminals was one of them; another was some rubbish about Degenerates. I am happy to say that I cannot even recall the author's name, but for months he bestrode Europe like a giant. As we are familiar with the material, so we are with the moral quality. For these books are very moral. They take no notice of nonsense like art for art's sake; indeed they take no notice of art at all. They have entirely reversed the narrow prejudice of the 'nineties against " a novel with a purpose ". This sort of creation never comes by accident; the crime was done on purpose. And its principle is that men must have a story with a moral; so long as it is not a moral moral. We all know the fictions in which people are allowed without limit to moralize against morality; against marriage or chivalry or personal honour. In these special cases the point was to moralize against national honour.

These books burst upon the world originally, to point out the little known fact that peril is perilous and pain is painful. But the thesis thrust upon us was not really the obvious thesis that war is heart-rending and horrible; it was the thesis that there is nothing noble about defying horror or enduring the rending of the heart. A justly popular English writer has been so much seized with this fanaticism, of denying any military virtues even as the accidents of military conditions, that he actually argued that most soldiers are safe to the point of monotony, and there is no risk to be represented as romance. To such a mental state does monomania

reduce even lively minds. It did not seem to occur
to him that he was abandoning the whole case against
war, in order to make a case against warriors. If
soldiers do not suffer, there is an end of all the huge
humanitarian movement against soldiering. And if
soldiers do suffer, it seems rather mean to deny them
even the credit of suffering. Logic of this type
debilitates most minds of this school. I remember
a critic who justified certain gross details in *All Quiet
on the Western Front*, on the ground that the world
ought to know the coarse conditions under which
soldiers had to live. Because unpleasant things ought
not to be public even in a camp, therefore they ought
to be published to the public. Because it is infamous
that they have no privacy on the battlefield, it is
admirable that they should have nothing but publicity
on the book-stall.

It is in a very different sense that a saner generation
will cover up such things in shame. It will recognise
all the horror involved in any case; but it will perhaps consider this sort of publicity the most horrible
thing. The time will most certainly come when we
shall be much more ashamed of the war-books than
of the war. Never before has such a laborious effort
been made to discredit even the desperate virtues,
with which man can confront the tragic accidents

The End of the Armistice

of his history. Another war book, of this pessimistic and paralysing intention, has been lately boomed, though with very much less success; and I do not propose to advertise it here. It is enough to say that it was taken up and advertised by one of the big capitalist newspapers; because the horrors it described were carefully confined to the French army. It thus became useful to that great propaganda in our press, which is dedicated to the dignified and enlightened end of abusing all foreigners. Foreign armies have mutineers; foreign armies contain cowards; foreign armies have panics or false accusations of panic; foreign armies have court-martials; and, being foreign court-martials, they are frightfully unjust. This is that carefully selected and exquisitely balanced combination of pacifism and patriotism, which now blooms in our press, and which by either name would smell as sweet. For my part I vastly prefer either howling jingoism or wild fanatical peace-at-any-price. The merit, and even the original sincerity, of books of this sort may vary a great deal; but neither could have given them the sort of practical importance that they have had. In a great many cases, the work partakes of the character of hack work. It exhibits the commonplace tragedy of all mass production; in its disproportion of responsibility. The important person in such a story is not the author but the publisher or the publicity man or the very uncritical critic. The only intellectual interest is in a new and abnormal motive; which is not so much a sense of tragedy as a hatred of anybody being made the hero of a tragedy. Hagiographers might overrate the torments of martyrdom; but nobody before ever wanted to underrate the martyrs.

XXXII

TORTURE AND THE WRONG TOOL

MR. HOFFMAN NICKERSON'S very stimu-
lating and even challenging book *Can We Limit
War?* recently published, contains many contro-
versial opinions with which many of his countrymen
will not agree, and some with which I do not agree
myself. But it contains one protest or warning,
touching the literature and journalism of our time,
with which I agree so warmly that I cannot refrain
from restating it; all the more strongly because
hardly anybody nowadays ever states it at all. It
concerns the choice of tools with which to work for
peace; a thing quite as practical as the choice of
weapons for waging war. Perhaps I might express
it myself, out of the depths of my morbid lust for
detective stories, by calling it a protest against the
Death-Ray Argument. We have all read shockers
and sensational stories, in which a white-haired and
wild-eyed Professor, alleged to be idealistic and
instantly recognised to be insane, is at work on pro-
ducing a Death-Ray or some deadly explosive or
destructive machine, so terrific as to lay the nations

Torture and the Wrong Tool

prostrate with panic, and thus achieve the happy result of imposing peace on the world. This cheery argument is repeated, in more realistic forms, in countless descriptions proving that the Next War will be so horrible that nobody will dare to wage it. Mr. Nickerson throws some healthy doubts on these nightmares; he questions whether a city like New York, for instance, could really be wiped out from the air as in the apocalyptic visions. He admits, in a passage of much truth and humour, that new tools do suffer from not being attached to old traditions. Savages poison arrows, but our civilisation always refused to poison wells; yet instantly agreed to poison gases. He adds that people who would be ashamed to shout or bang drums, to annoy their neighbours, do not care what they do with the radio. Nevertheless, we must not let our morals be really altered by our machinery. And what are we to say of the morals of people, who are only afraid to fight because somebody has got a Big Gun or towering engine of torture they cannot face? What *can* we say, except those hackneyed but very noble lines:

Cowards die many times before their death,
The valiant only taste of death but once.

The End of the Armistice

To remain at peace, out of sheer panic about a professor with a death-ray or a tyrant with an instrument of torture, would be indeed to die daily and even then not be secure against death.

I put it not as a point of politics but of culture and the current moral tone in literature. For instance, the one blot on Flecker's poetical play of *Hassan*, which contains some of the loveliest modern lyric poetry, is that it turns, not upon torture, but upon the triumph of torture. Now we poor traditional Christians, among whom Mr. Nickerson is to be numbered, have been abused for morbid martyrologies; " the ghastly glories of saints and dead limbs of gibbeted gods." But at least the darkest and most distorted Christian tales of torture did celebrate the triumph of the mind of man over torture. They did not congratulate the gridiron on conquering St. Lawrence; or bow down to the wheel because it broke the spirit of St. Catherine. Man has not yet been beaten by any engine of his own ; and I cannot comprehend anyone tolerating the idea that his story should end in such dishonour.

XXXIII

ON WAR AND PEACE

IT is expedient that we, who stand at the position,
now rapidly becoming isolated, of being ardent
lovers of peace (in common with the vast majority
of mankind through all the ages) without being
totally and babblingly ignorant of human nature or
of the course of human history, should pause on
occasion to define that position more narrowly.

Ten years ago at a critical period in the history
of Western civilization the direction of its destinies
fell into the hands of two men, the one an American
college professor, of excellent intention, but entirely
devoid of human sympathy; the other, a Welsh
demagogue. The one was concerned to devise a
paper scheme for the orderly regulation of international relations, a scheme perfect in its parts, and
eminently suitable for the government of angel-
races and dream-peoples; the other showed a fine,
careless disregard for what was done, so long as it
was productive of noise and notoriety and the front-
page "splash". Between them they concentrated
and established in a club-house at Geneva all the

The End of the Armistice

richest of the world's resources of amorphous idealism, a tribunal by constitution without authority and by composition without dignity. That done, they departed, the better man to his grave.

Because this organization of Geneva, impotent of action, has devoted itself principally in the last ten years to the intensive development of a pacifist propaganda campaign, it has come to be regarded in the public mind, by a common, unfortunate confusion of thoughts and things, ideas and institutions, as a symbol of world peace. Conversely, all those who find themselves out of sympathy with it, whether from a sense of historical proportion or from a simpler sense of the ludicrous, are in danger of being mistaken for protagonists of militarism. This is an impression which it has always been our endeavour to correct.

We do not hold, no sane man has ever held, that war is a good thing. It is better that men should agree than that they should disagree; it is better that they disagree peacefully than that they should fight. Thus far we go with the most ardent, unconditional pacifist. The horrors and abominations of war are not likely to be invoked. But we hold that occasion may arise when it is better for a man to fight than to surrender. War is, in the main, a dirty, mean, inglorious business, but it is not the direst calamity

that can befall a people. There is one worse state,
at least : the state of slavery.

While the possibility of slavery remains, while
it merges daily into imminent probability, it is more
important to teach men the value of manhood than
to preach the softer virtues of peace.

Anybody but a lunatic must agree that the dead
soldiers did their duty, or at least what they thought
was their duty ; and that they suffered in doing it.
We believe also that they fought for a just cause ; but
even if they did not, it would make no difference to the
duty or the suffering. But in that general break-up of
the brain, which seems to be following on the break-up
of the creed of Christendom, there has arisen out of the
deeps some diseased and half-witted fallacy ; according
to which the horror of the suffering contradicts the
heroism of the sufferers. We are not to admire heroes
because they endured horrors which only heroes could
endure. We are not to honour martyrs ; because
martyrdom hurts very much ; which was the only
reason for anybody honouring martyrs at all. And all
these contradictions are covered with some single phrase
such as "There is nothing glorious about war". There
is not much that is glorious about peace either, when
we use it in order to talk and think on that level.

XXXIV

THE PACIFIST AS PRUSSIANIST

I

THE other day, I met a Pole wandering in this
country; I think I should have known him for a
Pole, even before he spoke in that fine and fastidious
foreign English, which is so rapidly assimilated by
Poles. He had the keen face that is common among
his countrymen; for the Polish profile often cuts
the air like a combination of the axe and the eagle;
or the two faces of the carved sticks that are sold on
the mountain at Zakopane. But the most curious
thing about him was this; so curious that it seems
to me worthy of a note of further consideration, or
reconsideration, of the curious Continental position.
I saw him at a time when the whole world was
suddenly darkened by the vapour from the volcano
of the Nazi Revolution; when the nations had
turned pale under the threat of a new war; when
even the ordinary Pro-German had suddenly become
an Anti-Prussian; and felt that Poland and France
had every right to grow rigid with suspicion and
alarm. And in the midst of all this, and under-

neath this enormous shadow, the Pole was smiling. If he had been of a less delicate cultural tradition, I should say that he was grinning. He seemed to be almost the only person in England who was perfectly happy.

This fact interested me very much; and when he explained what he thought about things, it interested me still more. For it did reveal a very real fact, which I recognised for a fact, though I had myself forgotten it in the general excitement. The point of his position, roughly speaking, was this. " If the German Republic, the German Radicals and Rationalists, the German Socialists and Social Democrats, the Germans who put their faith in Progress, in Science, in all the everlasting enlightenment they talk about—if those liberal people had remained in power in Germany, all you people in England and America would have remained in sympathy with Germany. You would still be Pro-Germans, because the dear Germans would still be Progressives. You would back them up in anything they did, because they were such liberal and enlightened Germans. *Now, liberal and enlightened Germans hate Poland quite as madly as rough and reactionary Germans do.* German Socialists want to murder Poland quite as much as German militarists. German Jews want to murder it more." The trouble of the whole business, for those who do not understand Germany, is the fact that the strange self-worship of that strange people is really quite as strong in those who call themselves liberals because they are atheists, as in those who are honestly patriots making some attempt to remain Christians. Or rather more so. The more weak-kneed German Catholic may march a good part of the way with Prussianism; but he cannot actually reach the point of Paganism. The German Free-thinker need only take one step into complete Paganism. Even the Lutheran remembers that there was somebody before Luther; for whom Luther himself expressed some regard. And the ethnological proofs that Jesus Christ was a pure Nordic Teuton are not so satisfactory as was hoped. But the German sceptic can be completely sceptical about anyone who was not a German; and can put Luther as high above Christ as he likes. It is of the very nature of this new religion of Race that it flourishes better in a world of irreligion, than of anything that we used to call religion. And while the Catholic cannot merely hate Poles, and even the Lutheran may remember that somebody once asked him to love his enemies, the heathen can worship hatred just as he can worship lust. Therefore, said my Polish friend, it is really

The Pacifist as Prussianist

far better for us that Germany should be avowedly militaristic and reactionary; for then you will suspect and watch her; and possibly her next militarist move will be foiled after all. But, sooner or later, any Radical or Socialist German Government would have made a move of some sort against Poland; and it would have been backed up by all the silly simple-minded Radicals and Socialists and enlightened persons in the world.

Doubtless, this is only one aspect of the truth of a very bewildering situation; but it is important even apart from that particular situation. The world has heard a great many warnings against war, some of them very wise and well-balanced; but there is one particular warning which has not been emphasised half enough. It is the warning against the warlike potentialities of the Pacifists. In my experience, most Pacifists do not love their enemies; they only hate their friends for fighting against their enemies. Or rather, properly speaking, the enemies they forgive are really their friends; but they do not forgive those who are really their enemies. The kind of Pacifist who told us for the last ten years to be friendly to Germany would never in ten million years become friendly to France. He might not want to wage a war with France, in so far as it meant risking life, or

The End of the Armistice

losing money, or any of those things that are really wrong. He would not especially want to do it with any of the great military gestures, drawing the sword or unfurling the flag; for all that is very, very wrong. But he would not obstruct a war with France, as he obstructed a war with Germany. He would probably in practice support it, with normal civic and even military obedience. For he would always have at the back of his mind the notion that if it was a war against France, it was probably a war for Righteousness. For the international division is a religious division; and on the one side are those who fight for Righteousness and on the other those who fight for Justice. They are two different translations of the same Greek word; and their meanings in the modern world flatly contradict each other.

Do not altogether dismiss this danger of the Pacifist prejudice, the crypto-militarism of the internationalists; the wolf in sheep's clothing. He has counted for a great deal in Germany; and he may yet count for a great deal in England. During the War the German Socialists went into Belgium and actually used international arguments to whitewash the imperialistic oppression of the Belgians. There are any number of English Socialists who would be delighted to whitewash the imperialistic oppression of the Poles. But the more openly imperialistic the oppression is, the more difficult they will find it to whitewash it. The more brazen is Hitler's militarism, the less can the international idealist brazenly blow the Hitlerite trumpet. So perhaps there is something to be said for the paradox of my friend from Poland. And when we thank Hitler for some things at least, for stopping the nudist nonsense and burning *All Quiet on the Western Front*, we may add this to his merits ; that, by being so very military, he may have forced even Pacifists to keep the peace.

II

There is practically no doubt that the Pacifists have now for nearly twenty years been supporting Prussia. Only, for some time, they would have at least pretended that they were not supporting Prussianism. They believed, or professed to believe, that the North Germans had so suddenly and completely reversed all their recent traditions, that they had become the purely Pacifist element in Europe. And as North Germany is certainly the home of many freaks besides the freak of Teutonic tribal superiority, it was, of course, possible to produce examples on their side. It might be said that the Youth Movement, in which people went picnicking for indefinite periods, was more like a mild mutiny than a rigid militarism. It might be argued that the Prussian thinker, who walks about naked, has gone as far as anybody can in Disarmament.

The answer is that the Pacifist and the Prussianist fit each other as exactly—I was going to say as exactly as man and woman; but refrain for fear of a terrible and now tiresome argument about Sex. It would be truer to say that they are the active and passive mood of the same verb. A Pacifist is something which it is wise to be in the presence of a Prussianist. A Prussianist is something which it is safe to be in the presence of a Pacifist. Their common ground is that neither has any real idea of courage; neither has any notion of chivalry in war; just as neither the Capitalist nor the Communist has any idea of liberty in peace. They are in fact the ancient complex of the bully and the coward; always parts of the same operation and frequently, though proverbially, parts of the same person. For the Pacifist's idea of peace almost always involves a silent bullying; like the bullying of the poor by the police. And the Prussianist's idea of war has always a horrible atmosphere of peace; that is, of widely extended silence and discipline; of mechanical conquest and unquestioned occupation. I am not at all surprised that Prussianism and Pacifism have been in practice in alliance. Still, for the sake of logic and decency, there is still a question to be asked. Now that Prussia is again Prussian, and even Prussianist, what are the Pacifists going to say? Shall we hear a shout against Prussia—as now the manifest War-Maker of Europe?

And if not, why not?

XXXV

THE UMBRELLA QUESTION

IT is said that before the Flood men ate and drank
and married and gave in marriage ; but if they had
restricted themselves to these four most admirable
human habits, it is clear from the context that there
would never have been any Flood at all. On the
details of that primitive and probably very high
civilisation we need not speculate. Doubtless it
abounded in those abnormalities, which archæologists
discover and call very archaic, and moderns discover
and call very modern. But on some lighter aspects
we may make guesses about what probably happened
just before the Flood. For instance, a very rich man
who was feeling very well, because it was a fine day,
undoubtedly came out into the street and said in a
loud voice, " Rain is a thing of the past" (see *Life
of Andrew Carnegie, circa* 1912). Instantly after this,
with all the promptitude of an answer to prayer, a
heavy shower began to fall somewhere, and everybody came to the conclusion that it looked like rain.
Upon this a great and justly revered Prophet (who
had proved his power of piercing the future, by
saying that a primitive vehicle with one wheel like

a wheelbarrow, which had since been insecurely
balanced first on two wheels and then on three, would
probably end on four wheels and become a waggon)
issued an inspired proclamation to the whole earth,
which bore the title of " The Rain That Will End
Rain ". I need not pursue the rest of the rather
tragic story. There was a lull between the first big
storm and the second returning storm; and in this
interval various vigorous things were done. Leading
politicians in the chief commercial cities joined in a
Slogan; which was called, " We Have Outlawed
Rain ". But what occupied these politicians most
seriously was the question of the expenditure on
various instruments, of which the very existence
proved that men had still a craven fear that Rain
would someday return. What of the reckless expenditure on umbrellas ? What of the costly competition
between the umbrellas (nay, even the waterproofs)
of one city and another ? Had humanity really faced
as yet the frank generous policy of everybody throw-
ing away his umbrella ? Had we really in our hearts
that happy and consoling hope that nobody would
ever again want any umbrellas ? How much money
(they asked suddenly in tones of thunder) is even
now being spent on buying umbrellas ? This was the
only problem that occupied the politics and journalism

of all the cities of the earth, up to the exact moment when the Flood destroyed them all.

The example is ancient and familiar, which is why I choose it; for it does seem starkly incredible how the lighted foreground of life can continue idiotically identical, while the background changes so swiftly and darkens so terribly with tempest. As a point of abstract common sense, one would suppose it was clear enough; a man does not give up his umbrella at the exact moment when a thundercloud is threatening to crash over his head; a man does not give up his sword at the exact moment when his next-door neighbour, who has obviously gone mad, is waving sabres and battle-axes over the wall. It is a perfectly reasonable point of enquiry, in itself, whether steel is too expensive; or whether umbrellas are too large an item in any householder's expenditure. But to expect people to go on talking about nothing except the price of umbrellas during the steady increase of the Deluge, or to talk about nothing but the price of armaments under the instant threat of an appeal to arms, is simply not within the limits of human sanity. Yet it is the only topic recognised as really respectable in our national newspapers. It is horribly typical of such organs of opinion that they are always quite content with the continuity of a discussion, quite apart from whether there is ever any decision, or whether it is the wrong decision.

The Umbrella Question

So long as they hear that a consultation has not ended, they do not seem to care a curse about how it will end. It is a part of that strange mentality which loved to keep Problems as Problems, calling them the Drink Problem or the Slum Problem or the Sex Problem; they kept open problems like open wounds, and thought there was hope so long as they did not heal. So long as the doctors still discussed, they did not care if the doctors still disagreed. They now present to heaven and earth this huge and incredible incongruity of sitting down to discuss only whether we can save money on bombs and bayonets, and not whether we can save our lives from them.

The one solid advantage on our side is the fact that the man next door is not only a lunatic, but also a fool. A rain-cloud cannot help looking like rain, but a man meditating a sudden attack has no excuse for looking like a man meditating anything of the sort. If the German had really had any self-control, he might have done already what he is now wildly threatening to do, and equally wildly promising not to do. It makes him feel happy to wave a battle-axe even while explaining that he does not want a battle. Anything so weak-minded as that is always at a disadvantage, even when it is strongly armed ; even when it has hidden a hundred battle-axes in its house or backyard. The world will not forget the weird psychological effect of the Prime Minister of Prussia

215

shouting at a prisoner supposed to be receiving a fair trial, " You wait till I get you outside "; like a very low-class schoolboy threatening what he would do out of school. That sort of thing simply does not happen among civilised people; not even when they are very wicked people. How anybody can see such lunacy dancing in high places, in the broad daylight of political responsibility, and have any further doubt about the sort of danger that threatens the world, is more than I can understand. But some seem still to prefer to do a little quiet calculation, like a sort of cosmopolitan housekeeping, about whether General Goering could be induced to spend a little less on the spike on his helmet, if only General Castelnau could be induced to spend a little less on the spurs on his heels. Heaven knows our hope is not in our own rulers; or in most of the other rulers of the sophistical and secretive modern State. It is already becoming crudely obvious that our journalism juggles with the news. Even in the most respectable papers, great blocks of information will appear in one sheet and be utterly absent from the other; and next day be absent from both. We cannot put our trust in princes, or in the plutocrats who play the part of princes; we cannot trust entirely even our allies or our friends. But we can trust our enemy; we can put our faith in him; and know that he will not fail to go on proving our case.

XXXVI

CHRISTENDOM AND PRIDE

CHRISTENDOM, which is the only philosophical name of Europe, has been confronted in these last days with exactly the same problem which confronted it in its first days. It is loosely called the problem of Paganism ; but, when reduced to its realities, it will almost always be found, as I have already suggested, to be the problem of Pride. It was largely common both to the noble and the ignoble Pagans. It would be easy to maintain, for that matter, that the noble Pagans lived in the first days and the ignoble Pagans in the last. But such a generalisation is unjust—even to the ignoble Pagans of to-day. The historical question has been confused by exaggerations on both sides. We are accustomed of late to those who slander Christendom ; but there were some who did definitely slander Paganism. There did appear a sentimental type of Christian romance which implied that all early Christians were like Christ, and that all later Pagans were like Nero. To take this view is to miss the whole point of the mightiest revolution in the story of Man.

The greatest of Christian doctors were the first to admit that most of the Christian virtues had been heathen virtues. They only claimed that Christianity could alone really inspire a heathen to observe the heathen virtues. It is unjust to say that no heathens were ever merciful; it is absurd to say that no heathens were ever just. For that matter, there were heathen nuns and heathen vows of chastity; as in the Vestals or the cult of Diana. Upon one point and one point only, was there really a moral revolution that broke the back of human history. And that was upon the point of Humility. There was this definite thing about the best Pagan; that in him dignity did mean pride. It was a change that stood alone; and was worthy to stand alone. For it was the greatest psychological discovery that man has made, since man has sought to know himself.

It was the stupendous truth that man does not know anything, until he can not only know himself but ignore himself. He must subtract himself from the study of any solid and objective thing. As Swift profoundly said, the very definition of Honour is to " suppose the question not your own ". Vanity which is a pleasure, is a perfectly legitimate pleasure; like wine. But Pride, which is the falsification of fact, by the introduction of self, is the enduring blunder of mankind. Christianity would be justified if it had done nothing but begin by detecting that blunder. Now at this moment, that blunder is boiling up again on every side of us in Christendom; and threatening to whelm it again in barbarism.

The Centenary of the Oxford Movement gives only too many opportunities for recrimination and reproach; but in this at least all men who remember anything of its meaning may stand together. The great men of that movement lived at a moment when Pride in the Protestant countries like England was swollen to bursting, partly by vulgar wealth, partly also by healthy patriotism. It is amusing to read with what dazed derision the great Victorian like Thackeray or Dickens received its suggestions of returning to Penance or Mortification. Yet we have since seen the whole of that Victorian commercial England collapse as completely as Babylon or Carthage. It might be thought that other nations would learn that lesson, if only from us. But at the moment Pride, that monstrous and towering weakness, has risen again to do what it always does: to darken counsel, to confuse facts by confusing motives. We might applaud a hundred things done by the Nazis if we could bring ourselves to applaud the motive and the mood. Unfortunately it is a hysteria of self-praise, which is fed by its own virtues as much as its own vices. For that is the vital or rather mortal weakness of Pride. It says: "I did a fine thing kicking out a Jew usurer"; but it also says: "Bashing a Catholic boy scout was a fine thing, because I did it". It is in no partisan spirit that any Christian will smell evil in this vast explosion of gas and wind. Christendom has a new battle before it; no longer with the Lust that was called Liberty; no longer with the Scorn that was called Scepticism; no longer with the Envy that was called Divine Discontent; but with something much less mixed with sympathetic elements than any of these: with that primeval Spirit and Prince of the Powers of the world which it first came upon earth to defy. The Freethinkers of the future will care nothing for freedom and very little for thought. They will tell us that thought must be subject to will; and that will is whatever they want, or whatever they want it to be. The alliance between scepticism and democracy was wholly accidental; the new sceptics will be more sceptical of democracy than of anything else. They will be sceptical of everything and everybody except themselves. The Church will defend all that is left of democracy; as in the last century she defended all that was left of loyalty. A Pagan pride, freed from democratic as from religious restraints, is the next foe we have to face; and it may be hoped, in whatever form, that we shall all face it together.

EPILOGUE

RESURRECTION

IN our civilisation cities and realms do really rise
again; not merely when they have been defeated
but when they have been dead; not merely when
they have been at their weakest or their worst, but
when they have ceased to be. Everywhere else, in
the normal heathen life of humanity, there is either
continuity or else complete disappearance. Nobody
needs to restore a temple to Buddha in Burma;
because it has always been used by the Burmese.
But nobody hopes to restore a temple to Moloch
in Carthage; because Moloch has disappeared and
Carthage too. Where men still worship the gods
of Asia, those cults are continuous if sometimes a
little mechanical, like that of the last Pagan gods of
Europe. But no people worship the gods of Assyria;
and it is now impossible to imagine any people wanting to. But in Christendom there is an endless
revival of human things, and even of heathen things.
We do not believe that there are any lost causes;
we do not admit that there are any hopeless loyalties;
we do should come back to our religion at last, if
and we its temples were as deserted as Stonehenge.

The End of the Armistice

It is this splendour of the hopeless hope; sometimes called the forlorn hope, which has made the
peculiar chivalry of Christendom, which has given
to us alone the true idea of romance; for the real
romance was a combination of fidelity to the quest
as a task, with perpetual and enormous inequality
to the task. And if anyone wishes to know what is
really rooted in our religion, and typical of our
culture, he will find it in those late flowers and fruits
which have quite recently grown upon trees that
were counted utterly stricken and dead through the
long winters of recent centuries. He will see it in a
flash if he thinks for one moment of how short a
time separates the Irish Free State from the Irish
Famine; and when I went to Poland and heard again
the national march of the Poles, I told them that
through those words I heard words that were old
when all our songs were new, and shall be new when
all our songs are old: "I am the Resurrection and
the Life."